SPECTRUM®

Math

Grade 4

Published by Spectrum®
an imprint of Carson-Dellosa Publishing LLC
Greensboro, NC

Spectrum®
An imprint of Carson-Dellosa Publishing LLC
PO Box 35665
Greensboro, NC 27425 USA

© 2015 Carson-Dellosa Publishing LLC. Except as permitted under the United States Copyright Act, no partof this publication may be reproduced, stored, or distributed in any form or by any means (mechanically, electronically, recording, etc.) without the prior written consent of Carson-Dellosa Publishing LLC. Spectrum® is an imprint of Carson-Dellosa Publishing LLC.

Printed in the USA • All rights reserved.

ISBN 978-1-4838-0872-7

01-282177784

Table of Contents Grade 4

Chapter 1 Adding and Subtracting 1 and 2 Digits

Chapter 1 Pretest 5
Lessons 1–9 7–16
Chapter 1 Posttest 17

Chapter 2 Numeration through 1,000,000

Chapter 2 Pretest 19
Lessons 1–4 21–26
Chapter 2 Posttest 27

Chapter 3 Adding and Subtracting 3 through 5 Digits

Chapter 3 Pretest 29
Lessons 1–10 31–41
Chapter 3 Posttest 42

Chapter 4 Multiplication

Chapter 4 Pretest 44
Lessons 1–11 46–57
Chapter 4 Posttest 58

Chapter 5 Division

Chapter 5 Pretest 60
Lessons 1–10 62–74
Chapter 5 Posttest 75

Chapters 1–5 Mid-Test 77

Table of Contents, continued

Chapter 6 Fractions

Chapter 6 Pretest 83
Lessons 1–16 85–101
Chapter 6 Posttest 102

Chapter 7 Measurement

Chapter 7 Pretest 104
Lessons 1–17 108–124
Chapter 7 Posttest 125

Chapter 8 Geometry

Chapter 8 Pretest 129
Lessons 1–5 130–134
Chapter 8 Posttest 135

Chapter 9 Preparing for Algebra

Chapter 9 Pretest 136
Lessons 1–2 137–138
Chapter 9 Posttest 139

Chapters 1–9 Final Test 140

Scoring Record for Posttests, Mid-Test, and Final Test 146
Grade 4 Answers 147–159

Check What You Know

Adding and Subtracting 1 and 2 Digits

Add or subtract.

	a	b	c	d	e	f
1.	35 + 3	25 + 13	75 + 24	13 + 12	42 + 7	54 + 33
2.	43 + 24	54 + 5	63 + 31	82 + 16	32 + 23	74 + 15
3.	50 + 33	95 + 2	32 + 25	73 + 25	56 + 13	47 + 32
4.	12 + 7	36 + 12	55 + 23	70 + 19	92 + 4	54 + 23
5.	45 − 4	75 − 23	66 − 14	95 − 31	84 − 22	25 − 12
6.	49 − 27	57 − 46	39 − 18	79 − 27	27 − 6	88 − 56
7.	65 − 55	78 − 33	54 − 42	97 − 26	29 − 15	59 − 48
8.	54 − 23	29 − 18	47 − 37	99 − 66	89 − 27	36 − 15

NAME ______________________

Check What You Know

Adding and Subtracting 1 and 2 Digits

SHOW YOUR WORK

Solve each problem.

9. Mr. Dimas has 15 new students in his fourth-grade class. He already has 21 students in the class. How many students are in Mr. Dimas's class?

There are __________ students in his class.

9.

10. There are 35 pages in Kendrick's science book. Last night, Kendrick read 14 pages. How many more pages does Kendrick have left to read?

There are __________ pages left to read.

10.

11. Kono's father gave him 75 apples so he could pass them out to his friends. If Kono gave 43 away, how many apples does he have left?

There are __________ apples left.

11.

12. Monica and Tania want to throw a surprise party for Rosa. They plan to send out 45 invitations. If Tania writes 24, how many invitations does Monica need to write?

Monica needs to write __________ invitations.

12.

13. Seki's soccer team is in the State Cup Tournament. There were 23 goals made in the entire tournament. Seki's team made 12 of them. How many goals were made by the other teams?

The other teams scored __________ goals.

13.

NAME ______________________________

Lesson 1.1 Adding 1- and 2-Digit Numbers

addend →	6	60
addend →	+3	+30
sum →	9	90

If 6 + 3 = 9, then 60 + 30 = 90.

	Add the ones.	Add the tens.
23	23	23
+16	+16	+16
	9	39

Add.

	a	b	c	d	e	f
1.	11 + 8	10 +30	25 +14	81 +18	52 +17	74 +23
2.	10 +80	7 +2	15 + 4	7 +92	71 + 6	70 +10
3.	7 +22	20 +30	92 + 7	83 +16	46 +23	70 +20
4.	2 +41	30 +30	51 +48	34 +24	7 +22	20 +50
5.	30 +15	21 +21	7 +42	40 +40	56 +41	62 +17
6.	34 +34	60 +13	9 +30	4 +3	13 + 6	44 +33
7.	3 +32	5 +10	63 +24	71 +20	41 + 8	32 +30

NAME ______________________

Lesson 1.2 Subtracting 1- and 2-Digit Numbers

minuend →	9	90
subtrahend →	−3	−30
difference →	6	60

If 9 − 3 = 6, then 90 − 30 = 60.

	Subtract the ones.	Subtract the tens.
53 −21	53 −21 2	53 −21 32

Subtract.

	a	b	c	d	e	f
1.	33 −12	43 −20	91 −30	8 −3	90 −20	72 −11
2.	88 −24	59 −38	43 −31	50 −40	48 −17	72 −62
3.	25 −15	94 − 4	50 −30	35 − 3	27 −10	13 −12
4.	53 −40	14 − 3	18 −10	55 −42	9 −2	10 − 8
5.	49 −18	74 − 3	59 −27	68 − 7	93 −22	38 −37
6.	79 −35	21 −11	46 −42	78 −64	15 − 4	87 −35
7.	25 −13	71 −20	46 −23	56 −41	85 −63	99 −77

NAME ____________________

Lesson 1.3 Adding Three or More Numbers (single digit)

2 6 +7	→	8 + 7 15		
3 4 7 +1	→	7 7 +1	→	14 + 1 15

Add.

	a	b	c	d	e	f	g	h
1.	3 4 +5	2 6 +3	7 5 +3	6 3 +7	8 7 +2	9 8 +1	3 6 +8	1 7 +6
2.	4 6 +8	3 5 +2	1 5 +7	8 5 +3	4 7 +8	3 8 +9	2 6 +9	3 3 +7
3.	8 7 +5	8 3 +5	3 8 +2	2 8 +6	6 7 +8	3 6 +9	1 8 +7	5 7 +9
4.	1 3 5 +7	2 6 7 +4	1 5 9 +7	3 5 4 +6	2 2 2 +8	1 7 8 +9	4 4 5 +6	3 4 6 +8
5.	2 6 4 +8	2 2 8 +7	4 5 7 +9	3 3 4 +4	5 5 4 +3	6 3 7 +1	5 4 8 +9	1 7 1 +9
6.	9 1 7 +2	3 4 7 +8	2 5 7 +4	5 3 6 +5	8 3 9 +2	4 6 8 +3	7 3 7 +3	2 1 8 +5

NAME ____________________

Lesson 1.4 Adding through 2 Digits (with renaming)

	Add the ones.	Add the tens.
52 + 29	2 + 9 = 11 or 10 + 1; carry 1 → 52 + 29 = ?1	1 carried; 52 addend, +29 addend, 81 sum

Add.

	a	b	c	d	e	f
1.	36 + 15	29 + 18	57 + 23	18 + 13	74 + 6	8 + 27
2.	88 + 3	47 + 17	27 + 47	55 + 26	19 + 15	51 + 19
3.	65 + 26	39 + 39	25 + 25	45 + 45	36 + 48	75 + 16
4.	37 + 26	14 + 48	13 + 68	48 + 22	37 + 17	72 + 18
5.	65 + 25	9 + 48	7 + 77	82 + 9	28 + 9	48 + 32
6.	39 + 29	28 + 28	29 + 9	28 + 57	19 + 14	9 + 72
7.	75 + 7	73 + 9	36 + 36	78 + 18	19 + 19	43 + 17

NAME ____________________

Lesson 1.5 Adding Three or More Numbers (2 digits)

		Add the ones.	Add the tens.	
addend →	26	26 (carry 2)	26 (carry 2)	← addend
addend →	38	38	38	← addend
addend →	+56	+56	+ 56	← addend
		0	120	← sum

$6 + 8 + 6 = 20 \quad 20 = 20 + 0$

$20 + 20 + 30 + 50 = 120 \quad 120 = 100 + 20$

Add.

	a	b	c	d	e	f
1.	27 32 +43	39 48 +76	48 68 +78	97 85 +63	45 74 +48	97 23 +19
2.	77 99 +32	81 19 +38	53 78 +89	75 69 +78	38 57 +75	92 89 +95
3.	37 29 +49	87 78 +95	38 49 +57	42 28 +66	56 65 +77	19 37 +49
4.	35 73 57 +66	73 28 40 +66	88 22 38 +82	75 24 93 +51	29 93 37 +55	21 62 45 +38
5.	51 71 89 +99	20 18 39 +47	17 45 83 +97	27 58 74 +63	13 39 57 +89	57 33 71 +66
6.	39 29 58 +78	13 25 77 +89	27 53 68 +74	27 48 31 +97	22 17 39 +45	39 49 66 +77

NAME ____________________

Lesson 1.6 Subtracting 2 Digits from 3 Digits (renaming)

To subtract the ones, rename 5 tens and 3 ones as "4 tens and 13 ones."			Subtract the ones.	Subtract the tens.	Subtract the hundreds.
minuend →	153	⁴¹³ 1~~5~~~~3~~	⁴¹³ 1~~5~~~~3~~	⁴¹³ 1~~5~~~~3~~	⁴¹³ 1~~5~~~~3~~
subtrahend →	− 37	− 37	− 37	− 37	− 37
difference →			6	16	116

Subtract.

	a	b	c	d	e	f
1.	175 − 38	132 − 17	175 − 56	134 − 29	144 − 28	156 − 38
2.	182 − 73	177 − 59	123 − 18	141 − 33	173 − 54	182 − 48
3.	141 − 29	193 − 47	165 − 46	152 − 37	172 − 29	161 − 27
4.	183 − 68	127 − 18	134 − 19	172 − 57	124 − 17	153 − 37
5.	171 − 39	146 − 27	183 − 68	191 − 72	173 − 47	157 − 38
6.	128 − 19	172 − 36	156 − 29	177 − 39	152 − 19	174 − 38
7.	145 − 26	161 − 33	173 − 37	127 − 18	153 − 28	191 − 73

NAME ______________________

Lesson 1.6 Subtracting 2 Digits from 3 Digits (renaming)

	Rename 515 as "5 hundreds, 0 tens, and 15 ones." Subtract the ones.	Then, rename "4 hundreds, 10 tens, and 15 ones." Subtract the tens.	Subtract the hundreds.	
	0 15	4 10 15	4 10 15	
515	515	515	515	← minuend
− 27	− 27	− 27	− 27	← subtrahend
	8	88	488	← difference

Subtract.

	a	b	c	d	e	f
1.	138 − 59	162 − 79	155 − 66	128 − 59	147 − 58	174 − 85
2.	131 − 49	153 − 67	167 − 79	144 − 58	172 − 89	125 − 38
3.	114 − 37	134 − 56	181 − 92	133 − 44	127 − 49	174 − 88
4.	122 − 88	154 − 77	161 − 94	166 − 87	127 − 58	172 − 99
5.	177 − 88	123 − 45	147 − 68	181 − 95	175 − 89	141 − 83
6.	185 − 97	173 − 87	142 − 84	177 − 98	136 − 49	123 − 77
7.	127 − 58	126 − 78	166 − 89	137 − 88	153 − 84	175 − 97

NAME ____________________

Lesson 1.7 Thinking Subtraction for Addition

These numbers should be the same.

$$\begin{array}{r} 55 \\ +43 \\ \hline 98 \\ -43 \\ \hline 55 \end{array}$$

To check
55 + 43 = 98,
subtract 43 from 98.

Add. Then, check your answer.

	a	b	c	d	e	f
1.	$\begin{array}{r} 32 \\ +47 \\ \hline \\ - \\ \hline \end{array}$	$\begin{array}{r} 63 \\ +19 \\ \hline \\ - \\ \hline \end{array}$	$\begin{array}{r} 38 \\ +24 \\ \hline \\ - \\ \hline \end{array}$	$\begin{array}{r} 52 \\ +47 \\ \hline \\ - \\ \hline \end{array}$	$\begin{array}{r} 28 \\ +15 \\ \hline \\ - \\ \hline \end{array}$	$\begin{array}{r} 75 \\ +15 \\ \hline \\ - \\ \hline \end{array}$
2.	$\begin{array}{r} 48 \\ +27 \\ \hline \\ - \\ \hline \end{array}$	$\begin{array}{r} 82 \\ +10 \\ \hline \\ - \\ \hline \end{array}$	$\begin{array}{r} 56 \\ +38 \\ \hline \\ - \\ \hline \end{array}$	$\begin{array}{r} 44 \\ +27 \\ \hline \\ - \\ \hline \end{array}$	$\begin{array}{r} 28 \\ +27 \\ \hline \\ - \\ \hline \end{array}$	$\begin{array}{r} 39 \\ +32 \\ \hline \\ - \\ \hline \end{array}$
3.	$\begin{array}{r} 31 \\ +59 \\ \hline \\ - \\ \hline \end{array}$	$\begin{array}{r} 43 \\ +18 \\ \hline \\ - \\ \hline \end{array}$	$\begin{array}{r} 61 \\ +29 \\ \hline \\ - \\ \hline \end{array}$	$\begin{array}{r} 125 \\ +\ 17 \\ \hline \\ - \\ \hline \end{array}$	$\begin{array}{r} 155 \\ +\ 38 \\ \hline \\ - \\ \hline \end{array}$	$\begin{array}{r} 205 \\ +\ 69 \\ \hline \\ - \\ \hline \end{array}$
4.	$\begin{array}{r} 199 \\ +\ 14 \\ \hline \\ - \\ \hline \end{array}$	$\begin{array}{r} 128 \\ +\ 33 \\ \hline \\ - \\ \hline \end{array}$	$\begin{array}{r} 125 \\ +\ 50 \\ \hline \\ - \\ \hline \end{array}$	$\begin{array}{r} 109 \\ +\ 32 \\ \hline \\ - \\ \hline \end{array}$	$\begin{array}{r} 155 \\ +\ 27 \\ \hline \\ - \\ \hline \end{array}$	$\begin{array}{r} 137 \\ +\ 29 \\ \hline \\ - \\ \hline \end{array}$

NAME ______________________

Lesson 1.8 Thinking Addition for Subtraction

These numbers should be the same.

$$\begin{array}{r} 138 \\ -\ 24 \\ \hline 114 \\ +\ 24 \\ \hline 138 \end{array}$$

To check 138 − 24 = 114, add 24 to 114.

Subtract. Then, check your answer.

	a	b	c	d	e	f
1.	88 − 45	23 − 19	47 − 28	95 − 38	74 − 27	98 − 73
	+	+	+	+	+	+
2.	38 − 17	68 − 27	54 − 36	49 − 32	29 − 10	78 − 39
	+	+	+	+	+	+
3.	155 − 28	132 − 38	179 − 82	127 − 89	141 − 62	137 − 52
	+	+	+	+	+	+
4.	187 − 99	119 − 20	192 − 73	108 − 39	188 − 90	164 − 78
	+	+	+	+	+	+

NAME ______________________________

Lesson 1.9 Problem Solving

SHOW YOUR WORK

Solve each problem.

1. Isabel Jones needs to sell 175 calendars to raise money for the school band. She already sold 89 calendars. How many more calendars does she have to sell?

   She has to sell __________ more calendars.

2. Jacob Elementary School had a book drive. On Monday, the students collected 95 books. They collected 78 more books on Tuesday. How many books did the students collect?

   The students collected __________ books.

3. The Grover family went on a spring vacation. Their cabin is 305 miles away. If they drive 98 miles the first day, how many more miles do they have to drive to get to the cabin?

   They must drive __________ more miles.

4. The school cafeteria had an all-you-can-eat pizza party for the entire school. They made 215 slices of cheese pizza and 120 slices of pepperoni pizza. How many slices of pizza did they make?

   They made __________ slices of pizza.

5. There are 300 species of turtles and tortoises in the world. If there are 86 species listed as endangered, how many species of turtles and tortoises are not endangered?

   There are __________ species of turtles and tortoises that are not endangered.

1.
2.
3.
4.
5.

NAME ________________________

Check What You Learned

Adding and Subtracting 1 and 2 Digits

Add or subtract.

	a	b	c	d	e	f
1.	43 +27	57 +21	37 +15	73 +28	256 + 43	75 +25
2.	13 10 + 8	27 5 +23	238 + 68	91 82 +73	105 92 + 14	156 + 48
3.	21 +13	253 + 42	137 + 28	79 +97	103 + 18	65 +17
4.	73 21 +10	432 + 48	14 18 +32	66 +34	34 45 +57	13 +74
5.	245 − 32	105 − 16	35 −12	72 −28	91 −73	35 − 7
6.	107 − 34	94 −25	215 − 26	88 −49	173 − 28	72 −61
7.	35 −16	108 − 19	51 −32	125 − 15	199 − 84	84 −26
8.	147 − 48	62 −22	57 −32	111 − 12	123 − 48	92 −29

NAME ____________________

Check What You Learned

SHOW YOUR WORK

Adding and Subtracting 1 and 2 Digits

Solve each problem.

9. Tonya and her friends are collecting cans to recycle. Tonya has 55 cans, Irene has 32 cans, and Heather has 13 cans. How many cans do they have altogether?

They have __________ cans.

10. The football team is raising money by running a car wash. They need to wash 210 cars to raise enough money. They have washed 98 cars already. How many more cars do they need to wash?

They need to wash __________ more cars.

11. Ms. Brooks's science class is studying the environment around the school. Students counted 57 different plants and 25 different animals. How many plants and animals did the class find altogether?

The class found __________ plants and animals.

12. On a field trip, two sisters found frog eggs in a pond. Dee found 82 eggs and Shay found 118 eggs. How many frog eggs did they find?

They found __________ frog eggs.

13. At the bake sale, students brought in 115 cupcakes, 95 brownies, and 85 cookies. How many baked goods did the students bring in?

They brought in __________ baked goods.

9.
10.
11.
12.
13.

CHAPTER 1 POSTTEST

NAME ____________________

Check What You Know

Numeration through 1,000,000

Write each number in expanded form.

	a	b	c
1.	3,245	973	51
	______	______	______
2.	6,675	845,450	790
	______	______	______

Write the number word.

	a	b
3.	945	4,332
	______	______
4.	52,321	528,455
	______	______
5.	495,362	9,365,732
	______	______

Compare each pair of numbers. Write >, <, or =.

	a	b	c
6.	4,312 ___ 4,213	95 ___ 58	408 ___ 480
7.	52,650 ___ 52,560	610 ___ 672	72 ___ 62
8.	52,173 ___ 520,173	4,675,321 ___ 4,751,670	25 ___ 52
9.	158,325 ___ 158,325	652 ___ 256	8,910,003 ___ 8,910,003

CHAPTER 2 PRETEST

NAME ______________________

Check What You Know

Numeration through 1,000,000

SHOW YOUR WORK

Round each number to the place named.

	a	b	c
10.	7,649 thousands ______	932 hundreds ______	553,972 hundred thousands ______
11.	9,732,005 millions ______	75 tens ______	1,675 hundreds ______
12.	82,397 ten thousands ______	928 tens ______	682,349 thousands ______

Write the value of the 9 in each number.

	a	b	c	d
13.	95,235 ______	479 ______	1,976,235 ______	5,392 ______
14.	9,003,452 ______	2,349,003 ______	5,009,321 ______	8,793,215 ______
15.	6,000,942 ______	3,209 ______	794,367 ______	9,003,400 ______

NAME ______________________________

Lesson 2.1 Understanding Place Value (to hundreds)

Write each number in expanded form.

	a	b	c	d
1.	54 50 + 4	608	32	421
2.	430	549	75	699
3.	one hundred thirty-two	seven hundred twenty-one	thirty-nine	eighty-seven
4.	nine hundred eleven	five hundred thirteen	one hundred ninety	seventy

Write the numerical value of the digit in the place named.

	a	b	c	d
5.	872 tens 70	934 hundreds	326 ones	304 ones
6.	799 hundreds	663 tens	309 tens	995 hundreds

Write the number word.

7. 85,034

____

8. 11,987

____

NAME ______________________

Lesson 2.2 Understanding Place Value (to hundred thousands)

Write the number word.

1. 152,731

____

2. 985,685

____

Tell the digit in the place named.

	a	b
3.	50,975 ten thousands ________	986,580 hundred thousands ________
4.	179,802 thousands ________	506,671 ten thousands ________
5.	865,003 ten thousands ________	997,780 hundred thousands ________

Write each number in expanded form.

6.	653,410 ______________	76,982 ______________
7.	sixty-two thousand five hundred twelve ______________	103,254 ______________
8.	199,482 ______________	32,451 ______________

NAME ____________________

Lesson 2.3 Rounding

Round 15,897 to the nearest thousand.
Look at the hundreds digit. 15,<u>8</u>97

8 is greater than or equal to 5, so round 5 to 6 in the thousands place. Follow with zeros.

16,000

Round 234,054 to the nearest hundred.
Look at the tens digit. 234,0<u>5</u>4

5 is greater than or equal to 5, so round 0 to 1 in the hundreds place. Follow with zeros.

234,100

Round to the nearest ten.

	a	b	c	d	e	f
1.	6,421	5,882	45,288	975	13,936	842
	______	______	______	______	______	______
2.	9,855	26,917	984	95,645	8,673	29,981
	______	______	______	______	______	______

Round to the nearest hundred.

3.	325,793	49,832	123,652	24,635	199,794	79,342
	______	______	______	______	______	______
4.	798,759	58,345	9,873	8,375	10,097	1,987,654
	______	______	______	______	______	______

Round to the nearest thousand.

5.	567,523	93,567	4,378	12,499	747,399	9,385
	______	______	______	______	______	______
6.	987,436	346,436	98,345	8,564	75,459	187,349
	______	______	______	______	______	______

NAME ______________________

Lesson 2.3 Rounding

Round 783,538 to the nearest ten thousand. Look at the thousands digit. 78<u>3</u>,538 3 is less than 5, so keep 8 in the ten thousands place. Follow with zeros. 780,000	Round 2,895,321 to the nearest million. Look at the hundred thousands digit. 2,<u>8</u>95,321 8 is greater than or equal to 5, so round 2 to 3 in the millions place. Follow with zeros. 3,000,000

Round to the nearest ten thousand.

	a	b	c	d	e
1.	726,034	1,456,203	735,976	5,546,937	49,324
	______	______	______	______	______
2.	184,564	7,735,567	34,596	476,435	5,638,748
	______	______	______	______	______

Round to the nearest hundred thousand.

3.	4,835,694	354,543	9,325,987	7,952,436	456,987
	______	______	______	______	______
4.	8,745,123	1,057,251	435,900	9,730,204	576,132
	______	______	______	______	______

Round to the nearest million.

5.	7,499,887	6,576,362	2,245,984	4,458,876	7,561,110
	______	______	______	______	______
6.	1,935,761	3,666,345	7,468,994	5,565,740	8,089,768
	______	______	______	______	______

NAME ____________________

Lesson 2.4 Greater Than, Less Than, or Equal To

Inequalities are statements in which the numbers are not equal.

Compare 35 and 42.

35 < 42

Compare the values.
Look at the tens.
3 tens is less than 4 tens.
35 is less than 42.
This is an inequality.

< means "is less than."   > means "is greater than."   = means "is equal to."

Compare 110 and 112.

110 < 112

Compare the values.
Since the hundreds and tens are equal, look at the ones.
110 is less than 112.
This is an inequality.

Compare 55 to 55.

55 = 55

These numbers are equal, so this is not an inequality.

Compare each pair of numbers. Write >, <, or =.

	a	b	c
1.	105 ___ 120	52 ___ 35	10,362 ___ 10,562
2.	5,002 ___ 2,113	713 ___ 731	12,317 ___ 11,713
3.	115,000 ___ 105,000	23 ___ 32	142 ___ 142
4.	310 ___ 290	715 ___ 725	1,132,700 ___ 1,032,700
5.	616 ___ 106	119,000 ___ 120,000	48,112 ___ 48,212
6.	823 ___ 821	2,003,461 ___ 2,004,461	7,903 ___ 9,309
7.	30 ___ 25	47,999 ___ 45,999	19,900 ___ 19,090
8.	111 ___ 111	386,712 ___ 386,711	615 ___ 614

NAME ____________________

Lesson 2.4 Greater Than, Less Than, or Equal To

Compare the numbers. Write <, >, or =.

4,326 _>_ 4,226

This statement is called an **inequality** because the two numbers are not equal.

Look at the hundreds. 3 hundreds is greater than 2 hundreds.

Compare each pair of numbers. Write >, <, or =.

	a	b	c
1.	3,647 ___ 36,647	4,678 ___ 4,768	68,035 ___ 68,025
2.	4,102,364 ___ 4,201,364	56,703 ___ 56,702	125,125 ___ 125,150
3.	90,368 ___ 90,369	5,654,308 ___ 5,546,309	65,003 ___ 65,013
4.	4,567,801 ___ 456,780	7,621 ___ 7,261	769,348 ___ 759,348
5.	506,708 ___ 506,807	1,365,333 ___ 1,365,333	9,982 ___ 9,928
6.	224,364 ___ 234,364	32,506 ___ 23,605	7,850 ___ 7,850
7.	3,204,506 ___ 3,204,606	9,851 ___ 9,850	2,000,567 ___ 2,001,567
8.	430,632 ___ 480,362	49,984 ___ 49,984	5,640,002 ___ 5,639,992
9.	172,302 ___ 173,302	212,304 ___ 212,304	6,886 ___ 6,896

NAME ______________________

Check What You Learned

Numeration through 1,000,000

Write each number in expanded form.

	a	b
1.	1,965,012	693,145
2.	103,458	23,972
3.	471,440	18,321
4.	98,485	313,082

Write the number word for each number given.

	a	b	c	d
5.	5,012	102	1,141	99,612
6.	218	21,812	7,982	762
7.	456	123	934,763	37,103

CHAPTER 2 POSTTEST

NAME ____________________

Check What You Learned

Numeration through 1,000,000

Round each number to the nearest ten thousand.

	a	b	c	d	e
8.	2,396,473	763,465	85,123	2,391,362	625,104
	______	______	______	______	______
9.	305,419	8,939,721	434,599	49,002	2,009,452
	______	______	______	______	______

Round each number to the nearest hundred thousand.

10.	2,952,430	783,210	3,085,997	876,520	385,921
	______	______	______	______	______
11.	509,815	7,651,298	198,205	6,519,190	457,213
	______	______	______	______	______

Round each number to the nearest million.

12.	2,456,997	9,352,697	6,976,542	4,561,004	7,395,467
	______	______	______	______	______
13.	1,596,412	7,396,732	9,235,987	3,396,374	5,564,320
	______	______	______	______	______

Compare each pair of numbers. Write >, <, or =.

	a	b	c
14.	24,124 ___ 24,224	1,975,212 ___ 1,985,212	56,410 ___ 54,408
15.	509,712 ___ 590,172	2,341,782 ___ 2,341,782	976,152 ___ 967,932
16.	6,918 ___ 6,818	49,917 ___ 49,907	3,425,556 ___ 3,524,565
17.	8,724,100 ___ 5,724,101	3,002,019 ___ 3,002,109	2,418 ___ 2,418

NAME ______________________

Check What You Know

Adding and Subtracting 3 through 5 Digits

Add.

	a	b	c	d	e
1.	562 + 217	1452 + 519	732 + 195	3721 + 146	5605 + 1324
2.	4003 + 1717	193 + 117	2281 + 1307	624 + 624	1502 + 375
3.	443 + 237	5127 + 310	6152 + 1343	9730 + 169	1070 + 910
4.	3489 + 1301	2811 + 1187	6423 + 314	900 + 134	3007 + 2993

Subtract.

	a	b	c	d	e
5.	2817 − 314	987 − 445	7760 − 1352	583 − 472	9057 − 3152
6.	8648 − 526	9382 − 7481	5533 − 4622	7520 − 1418	4103 − 136
7.	5799 − 3182	2872 − 591	1890 − 727	2378 − 1060	22486 − 475
8.	972 − 175	7003 − 1762	834 − 514	71487 − 2271	9772 − 379

NAME ____________________

Check What You Know

SHOW YOUR WORK

Adding and Subtracting 3 through 5 Digits

Solve each problem.

9. Pablo and his family love to travel. This summer, they traveled 2,433 miles to visit relatives. If Pablo's family traveled 1,561 miles last year, how many miles have they traveled in the past two years?

They traveled __________ miles in the past two year?

10. The Brown County Humane Society took in 15,538 pets in the first six months of the year. The rest of the year, they took in 10,456 pets. How many pets did they take in during the year?

They took in __________ pets during the year.

11. Springfield School District bought 578 new science books. There are 1,976 students in the science classes. How many students will not receive a new book?

There will be __________ students without a new book.

12. Yoki had to ride a bus for 1,472 miles to get to Ashland City. The bus broke down after 1,227 miles. How many more miles did Yoki have to travel?

He had __________ miles left to travel.

13. Trey is getting ready to go to basketball camp. There are 213 players arriving on Friday and 131 players arriving on Saturday. If Trey arrives on Sunday with 104 more players, how many players will be at the camp?

There will be __________ players at the camp.

9.
10.
11.
12.
13.

NAME ______________________

Lesson 3.1 Adding 3-Digit Numbers

Add the ones.	Add the tens.	Add the hundreds.
256 +253 9	1 256 +253 09	1 256 ← addend +253 ← addend 509 ← sum

Add.

	a	b	c	d	e	f
1.	727 +182	503 +247	482 +107	132 +127	663 +125	823 +170
2.	337 +224	281 +127	407 +313	557 +223	487 +111	723 +432
3.	804 +179	198 +198	374 +298	503 +307	413 +344	723 +177
4.	652 +328	298 +133	511 +347	734 +536	309 +403	178 +131
5.	733 +156	543 +123	317 +226	199 +188	904 +396	825 +125
6.	902 +112	284 +173	610 +330	448 +136	709 +148	138 +125
7.	700 +493	509 +409	822 +188	294 +103	956 +143	248 +109

NAME ____________________

Lesson 3.2 Subtracting through 4 Digits

Subtract the ones.	Rename and subtract the tens.	Rename and subtract the hundreds.
1748 − 952 6	6 14 1748 − 952 96	16 0 6 14 1748 ← minuend − 952 ← subtrahend 796 ← difference

Subtract.

	a	b	c	d	e	f
1.	3621 −2710	947 −338	1479 − 346	403 −172	5521 − 725	800 −401
2.	5347 − 849	1763 −1452	937 −647	6633 −3366	710 −607	4036 −2072
3.	2786 −1684	475 −285	7036 − 936	888 −364	1010 − 909	1505 − 436
4.	8287 − 475	432 −151	4675 −3765	1403 − 647	872 −721	6483 −4894
5.	2440 −2332	5280 −2502	5420 −1938	992 −367	5678 −1234	3146 − 454
6.	2535 −2312	4311 − 564	7653 −1953	1992 − 741	5244 −2631	7198 −2112

NAME ______________________

Lesson 3.3 Adding 4-Digit Numbers

Add the ones.	Add the tens.	Add the hundreds.	Add the thousands.	
1564	1564	1564	1564	← addend
+4322	+4322	+4322	+4322	← addend
6	86	886	5886	← sum

Add.

	a	b	c	d	e
1.	1576 +1321	4009 +1019	2806 +1404	7314 +3728	6410 +2302
2.	3309 +2190	5754 +3475	5732 +4260	2895 +1435	7311 +1695
3.	5094 +1557	3150 +1472	1949 +1799	2473 +1303	2487 +1658
4.	1887 +1884	2797 +2613	2005 +2023	7300 +1795	6114 +1876
5.	3113 +2002	1720 +2071	4025 +1883	5758 +3837	6754 +1006
6.	7430 +2670	3552 +4431	3020 +4070	1448 +1336	8467 +1452
7.	8970 +5732	1776 +1406	5123 +3011	2882 +1999	4909 +2080

NAME ______________________________

Lesson 3.4 Problem Solving

SHOW YOUR WORK

Solve each problem.

1. A moving company moved 3,400 families this year. Last year, the company moved 2,549 families. How many families did the company move in the past two years?

   The company moved ________ families.

2. The Buckton Pet Store buys a total of 7,307 crickets every month for lizard food. If the store needs 230 crickets per month to feed their own lizards, how many crickets are left to sell to customers?

   They have ________ crickets left to sell to customers.

3. James and Curtis entered a bike racing event. There were 121 people entered in the event and 240 people watching. How many people were there in all?

   There were ________ people at the event.

4. The football team at Franklin High weighed in at 2,150 pounds. The football team at Union High weighed in at 2,019 pounds. How much more did the Franklin High team weigh?

   The Franklin High team weighed ________ pounds more.

5. Southgate Nursery sold 561 flowers on Saturday and 359 flowers on Sunday. How many flowers did Southgate Nursery sell over the weekend?

   Southgate Nursery sold ________ flowers.

6. In one morning, workers picked two loads of corn from the fields. The first load weighed 1,558 pounds and the second load weighed 1,600 pounds. How many pounds of corn did the workers pick that morning?

   The workers picked ________ pounds of corn.

1.
2.
3.
4.
5.
6.

NAME ______________________

Lesson 3.5 Subtracting 4- and 5-Digit Numbers

Subtract the ones.	Subtract the tens.	Rename and subtract the hundreds.	Rename and subtract the thousands.	
		2 15	0 12 15	
13546	13546	13546	13546	← minuend
− 7643	− 7643	− 7643	− 7643	← subtrahend
3	03	903	5903	← difference

Subtract.

	a	b	c	d	e
1.	25625 − 6510	73461 − 3861	40305 − 6307	15898 − 4775	66859 − 34437
2.	80247 − 15136	33969 − 20979	95348 − 6007	59109 − 45207	82468 − 3547
3.	45244 − 45227	63207 − 8009	77528 − 68431	10826 − 2715	57578 − 23888
4.	22127 − 3125	50003 − 15102	85713 − 7649	27791 − 13782	84875 − 74046
5.	99818 − 66919	39000 − 8007	19909 − 8723	29301 − 15082	13109 − 11008
6.	10806 − 6090	42875 − 33705	30000 − 15000	24080 − 16427	16046 − 8204
7.	76115 − 24007	87223 − 8224	24955 − 13865	30080 − 2400	67660 − 55084

NAME ____________________

Lesson 3.6 Adding 3 or More Numbers (through 4 digits)

Add each place value from right to left.

3251	2456
335	3210
+ 248	410
	+ 235
3,834	6,311

Add.

	a	b	c	d	e
1.	460 240 16 + 14	300 305 240 + 65	605 245 113 +105	600 42 36 + 29	1324 720 310 + 209
2.	6410 4205 +3112	812 16 + 12	7615 1207 +1152	617 522 +113	2012 150 + 150
3.	1935 1690 130 + 117	9132 7516 1509 + 123	5903 4051 1230 +1005	7213 4132 3715 +1503	942 483 305 +236
4.	5017 1243 + 502	8800 5008 +4112	1725 1528 +1341	7525 5150 +1000	4973 2007 +1221
5.	3417 2345 1132 + 305	5009 4103 2705 +1003	4107 3224 1115 + 607	7010 5528 3175 + 948	5139 4722 1056 +1013

NAME ____________________

Lesson 3.7 Adding 4- and 5-Digit Numbers

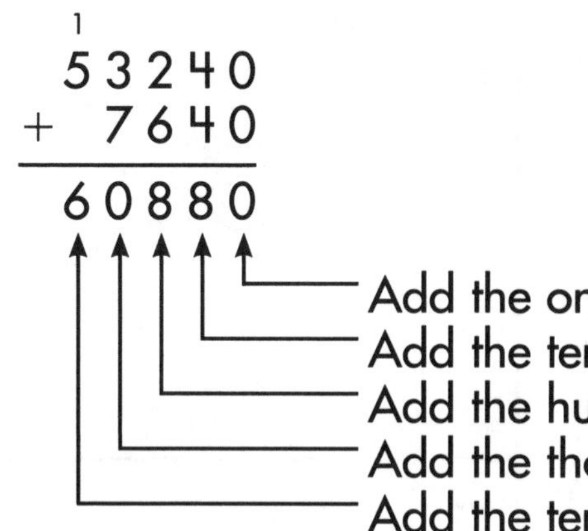

Add the ones.
Add the tens.
Add the hundreds.
Add the thousands.
Add the ten thousands.

53240 ← addend
+ 7640 ← addend
60880 ← sum

Add.

	a	b	c	d	e
1.	4301 + 7256	23125 + 1150	7372 + 1727	74323 + 28057	2248 + 1184
2.	23703 + 6147	9100 + 3498	13788 + 9093	5009 + 5009	10735 + 5781
3.	5112 + 3227	45173 + 3217	4880 + 2009	25883 + 24458	82048 + 8953
4.	10738 + 1327	8327 + 2735	64576 + 13610	7993 + 6814	23230 + 17075
5.	2376 + 1484	33782 + 5118	9109 + 4701	40119 + 25118	7594 + 3505
6.	14157 + 3352	5213 + 3004	32705 + 18805	2484 + 1555	15978 + 14605

NAME ______________________

Lesson 3.8 Problem Solving

SHOW YOUR WORK

Solve each problem.

1. Last year, 5,670 teenagers lived in Perry County. This year, 732 more teenagers moved there. If 2,115 more teenagers move in, how many teenagers will live in Perry County?

   There will be __________ teenagers living in Perry County.

2. There are about 5,400 species of mammals in the world. There are about 10,000 species of birds. About how many mammals and birds are there in the world?

   There are __________ species of mammals and birds.

3. Mi-Ling and Chet Ai are interested in the planets. They found out Saturn is about 72,367 miles wide and Earth is about 7,918 miles wide. How much wider is Saturn?

   Saturn is __________ miles wider.

4. Over the weekend, the Midmark Theater sold 1,208 buckets of popcorn, 2,543 sodas, and 973 boxes of candy. How many food items did the theater sell?

   The theater sold __________ food items.

5. At the state fair, the candy booth was very popular. It had a swimming pool filled with chocolate-covered peanuts and pretzels. There was a total of 97,635 pieces of candy in the pool. The pool had 56,784 chocolate-covered peanuts. How many pretzels were there?

   There were __________ pretzels.

1.

2.

3.

4.

5.

NAME ____________________

Lesson 3.9 Addition and Subtraction Practice

Add.

	a	b	c	d	e
1.	39741 + 4372	75103 + 1789	34396 + 33715	60056 + 13051	9408 + 2592
2.	1515 + 1212	10763 + 9275	66804 + 32198	2575 + 1984	25788 + 17875
3.	13362 + 44202	45245 + 2163	74612 + 3400	45220 + 1399	4998 + 3975
4.	371 + 287	2513, 727 + 236	937 + 793	815, 673 + 295	7035, 1293 + 713

Subtract.

	a	b	c	d	e
5.	5703 − 2147	13817 − 7616	1215 − 130	36973 − 19782	7113 − 6327
6.	79342 − 7983	44500 − 24712	6137 − 4372	60704 − 50913	9702 − 7512
7.	8791 − 370	3487 − 1807	55013 − 5907	47893 − 45797	8119 − 795
8.	84003 − 26174	19834 − 9796	39137 − 25126	6655 − 4837	7841 − 957

NAME ____________________

Lesson 3.9 Addition and Subtraction Practice

Add.

	a	b	c	d	e
1.	6418 527 + 318	1385 972 + 113	5759 2132 + 784	9107 6048 + 710	1248 1212 +1047
2.	998 +795	10007 + 9323	72457 +38718	6514 +3572	105 +103

Subtract.

3.	8080 −4092	79998 −37948	47973 − 9007	7013 −6912	8173 −7289
4.	18873 −12092	51135 − 2076	5117 −4108	1195 − 945	7495 −6816

Add or subtract.

5.	4405 + 758	66481 − 8675	4007 −3216	12489 + 7981	2817 − 250
6.	341 +298	17116 + 8713	97581 −85762	6245 +5345	15035 − 7335
7.	14809 −12734	28785 +13816	9248 −4517	5217 +5172	92408 − 8862
8.	4500 3217 +2518	87672 −69318	5218 735 + 613	6208 +1517	7185 5807 + 914

NAME ________________________________

Lesson 3.10 Problem Solving

SHOW YOUR WORK

Solve each problem.

1. Roberto and Steve counted the pennies they have been saving for 5 years. Roberto has 52,781 pennies and Steve has 58,972 pennies. How many pennies do they have altogether?

They have __________ pennies.

1.

2. A baseball team gave away free hats to 10,917 fans. There were 13,786 people at the game. How many fans did not get a free hat?

__________ fans did not get a free hat.

2.

3. Mr. Chien's art classes melted down broken crayons to make a wax figure. The morning class melted 7,325 pieces. The afternoon class melted 6,800 pieces. How many pieces did the classes melt?

The classes melted __________ pieces.

3.

4. There are 5,248 different types of insects in Sue's neighborhood. Of those, 518 can be harmful to people. How many insects cannot hurt Sue?

__________ insects cannot hurt Sue.

4.

5. Jasmine and her brother counted their button collection. Jasmine counted 5,213 buttons in all. Her brother counted 973 buttons that were blue. How many buttons were not blue?

__________ buttons were not blue.

5.

6. The post office delivered 55,002 letters to pen pals in England this year. Last year, the post office delivered 49,000 letters. How many more letters did the post office deliver this year?

The post office delivered __________ more letters this year.

6.

NAME ______________________

Check What You Learned

Adding and Subtracting 3 through 5 Digits

Add or subtract.

	a	b	c	d	e
1.	89700 + 9313	49713 + 13169	790 + 304	1825 + 775	7914 + 308
2.	15431 + 10917	50012 + 1597	2118 + 825	7381 + 5964	52005 + 8007
3.	735 + 162 + 94	6280 + 3770	2515 + 1003 + 714	68810 + 43057	8291 + 6104 + 5596
4.	68045 − 7210	3815 − 2756	22816 − 18792	7892 − 993	68613 − 40007
5.	66891 − 9073	99895 − 75872	7001 − 6342	9723 − 714	26819 − 7910
6.	2519 − 1943	1050 − 713	70462 − 70210	51372 − 8619	38982 − 17551
7.	52873 + 3219	4872 + 1356	80972 + 7321	7298 + 753	48932 + 30942
8.	4962 − 519	59782 − 53973	87752 − 8521	7495 − 6581	9325 − 2513

CHAPTER 3 POSTTEST

NAME ______________________

Check What You Learned

SHOW YOUR WORK

Adding and Subtracting 3 through 5 Digits

Solve each problem.

9. Reva's doctor wants her to walk more for exercise. She has to walk 10,000 steps daily. On Saturday, she only walked 8,972 steps. How many more steps did Reva need to walk?

   She needed to walk ________ more steps.

10. Curtis wanted to paint his bedroom either blue or green. At the paint store, there were 785 shades of blue and 685 shades of green. How many color choices did Curtis have?

    Curtis had ________ color choices.

11. Clare collects stamps from around the world. She has 2,315 stamps so far, but her goal is to have 5,500 stamps. How many more stamps does she need to complete her collection?

    She needs ________ more stamps.

12. John's brother is in high school and needs to write a 1,500-word report on pollution. He has 842 words in the report so far. How many more words does he need?

    He needs ________ more words.

13. The hospital's service elevator can hold 12,560 pounds. A technician and equipment weigh 752 pounds. How much more weight can the elevator hold?

    The elevator can hold ________ more pounds.

9.

10.

11.

12.

13.

NAME ______________________

Check What You Know

Multiplication

Multiply.

	a	b	c	d	e	f
1.	7 × 8	25 × 3	302 × 13	17 × 15	10 × 9	12 × 12
2.	315 × 47	9 × 9	91 × 52	32 × 33	403 × 7	93 × 8
3.	605 × 40	79 × 21	100 × 22	1,219 × 8	117 × 23	49 × 8
4.	750 × 23	10 × 10	794 × 2	75 × 25	11 × 11	972 × 3
5.	452 × 92	88 × 22	3,211 × 6	66 × 7	78 × 73	802 × 16

Write the factors of each number. Then, label it *prime* or *composite*.

		Factors	**Prime or Composite?**
6.	12	______________	______________
7.	11	______________	______________
8.	20	______________	______________
9.	32	______________	______________

NAME ___________________________

Check What You Know

Multiplication

SHOW YOUR WORK

CHAPTER 4 PRETEST

Solve each problem.

10. Students set up the chairs for the spring concert at Bethel High School. There were 25 rows with 10 chairs in each row. How many chairs did they set up?

They set up __________ chairs.

10.

11. The school carnival was a success. The school sold 99 tickets and each ticket was good for 2 rides. How many rides did the school sell?

The school sold __________ rides.

11.

12. At the Bead Shop, there are 25 rows of glass beads. If there are 320 glass beads in each row, how many glass beads are in the shop?

There are __________ glass beads in the shop.

12.

Write the equation. Then, solve each problem.

13. The cafeteria planned to bake 3 chocolate chip cookies for every student in the school. If there are 715 students, how many cookies does the cafeteria need to bake?

The cafeteria needs to bake __________ cookies.

13.

14. Crystal and Eva have been working 10 hours every week on their oral report on Rosa Parks. If they work on the report for 5 weeks, how many hours will they work on the report?

They will work __________ hours on the report.

14.

NAME ____________________

Lesson 4.1 Prime and Composite Numbers

A number is called **prime** if its only factors are 1 and itself.

For example, 7 is a prime number. The only factors of 7 are 1 and 7.

A number is called **composite** if it has more than two factors.

For example, 8 is a composite number. 1, 2, 4, and 8 are all factors of 8.

List the factors of each number. Then, label each number as *prime* or *composite*.

		Factors	Prime or Composite?
1.	64	____________	____________
2.	43	____________	____________
3.	53	____________	____________
4.	72	____________	____________
5.	19	____________	____________
6.	48	____________	____________
7.	22	____________	____________
8.	36	____________	____________
9.	89	____________	____________
10.	31	____________	____________
11.	93	____________	____________
12.	75	____________	____________

NAME ____________________

Lesson 4.1 Prime and Composite Numbers

List the factors of each number. Then, label each number as *prime* or *composite*.

		Factors	**Prime or Composite?**
1.	80	________	________
2.	55	________	________
3.	28	________	________
4.	67	________	________
5.	88	________	________
6.	73	________	________
7.	54	________	________
8.	95	________	________
9.	18	________	________
10.	91	________	________
11.	57	________	________
12.	13	________	________
13.	61	________	________
14.	77	________	________
15.	33	________	________
16.	23	________	________

NAME ______________________

Lesson 4.2 Interpreting Equations

SHOW YOUR WORK

Write the equation. Then, solve the problem.

1. Reid is 3 years old. His sister is 4 times older. How old is Reid's sister?

   She is ____12____ years old.

2. Tia has 7 hair bows. Her sister has 6 times as many as Tia. How many hair bows does Tia's sister have?

   She has __________ hair bows.

3. Jay mows 1 lawn every day Monday through Saturday. He is paid $25 for each lawn. How much money does Jay earn mowing lawns?

   Jay earns $ __________.

4. Macon eats 33 animal crackers as a snack every day after school. How many animal crackers does he eat during a 5-day school week?

   He eats __________ animal crackers.

5. Melanie bought 7 packages of greeting cards. Each package had 9 cards. How many greeting cards did she get in all?

   She got __________ greeting cards.

6. Chris walked 4 miles a day for 21 days. How many miles did he walk in all?

   He walked __________ miles.

Show your work:

1. $3 \times 4 = a$

   $a = 12$

2.

3.

4.

5.

6.

NAME ___________________________

Lesson 4.3 Multiplying 2 Digits by 1 Digit

$$\begin{array}{r} 32 \\ \times\ 3 \\ \hline 6 \end{array}$$ Multiply 2 ones by 3. $2 \times 3 = 6$

$$\begin{array}{r} 32 \\ \times\ 3 \\ \hline 96 \end{array}$$ Multiply 3 tens by 3. $30 \times 3 = 90$

Multiply.

	a	b	c	d	e	f
1.	23×2	71×1	12×4	33×2	10×7	24×2
2.	44×2	43×2	90×1	22×4	12×3	14×2
3.	11×9	75×1	11×6	30×3	10×4	42×2
4.	11×7	10×2	33×0	13×3	20×3	31×2
5.	10×2	41×2	13×2	40×2	30×2	11×5
6.	30×1	11×7	25×1	42×0	22×3	10×1
7.	14×0	10×5	31×3	12×3	20×4	10×7

NAME ______________________

Lesson 4.4 Multiplying 2 Digits by 1 Digit (renaming)

$$\begin{array}{r} \overset{1}{7}2 \\ \times\ 8 \\ \hline 6 \end{array}$$

Multiply 2 ones by 8.
$2 \times 8 = 16$ or $10 + 6$

6 ← Put 6 under the ones place.
Add the 10 above the 7.

$$\begin{array}{r} \overset{1}{7}2 \\ \times\ 8 \\ \hline 576 \end{array}$$

Multiply 7 tens by 8.
Then, add 1 ten.

$70 \times 8 = 560 \rightarrow 560 + 10$
$= 570$ or $500 + 70$

Multiply.

	a	b	c	d	e	f
1.	73×4	25×2	36×3	52×5	23×4	42×5
2.	19×2	26×2	68×3	54×5	47×8	33×4
3.	32×9	48×8	52×3	34×4	17×5	22×5
4.	66×3	45×5	66×5	19×9	38×9	74×3
5.	55×3	64×8	83×5	49×7	50×9	86×6
6.	60×6	17×3	48×9	75×3	60×9	96×5
7.	31×9	77×4	82×3	96×3	40×7	79×2

NAME ___________________________

Lesson 4.5 Problem Solving

SHOW YOUR WORK

Solve each problem.

1. There are 48 chicken farms near an Ohio town. If each farm has 9 barns, how many total barns are there?

   There are __________ total barns.

2. Mr. Ferris has a canoe rental business. Over the weekend, he rented 47 canoes. A canoe holds 3 people. If each canoe was full, how many people did Mr. Ferris rent to over the weekend?

   Mr. Ferris rented to __________ people.

3. The school planned for 92 students to attend the school dance. The school bought 4 slices of pizza for each student. How many slices did the school buy?

   The school bought __________ slices.

4. The pool opened on Memorial Day. Ninety-four people showed up. The pool manager gave out 2 vouchers to each person for free drinks. How many vouchers did the pool manager give out?

   The manager gave out __________ vouchers.

5. In the Sumton community, there are 56 houses. If there are 3 children living in each house, how many children live in houses in Sumton?

   There are __________ children living in houses in Sumton.

6. Deon and Denise are saving up to buy a computer game. If they put 23 dollars a week in the bank, how much money will they have in 5 weeks?

   They will have __________ dollars.

1.
2.
3.
4.
5.
6.

NAME ______________________

Lesson 4.6 Multiplying 3 Digits by 1 Digit (renaming)

$$\begin{array}{r} \overset{1}{7\,5}\,2 \\ \times \quad 8 \\ \hline 6 \end{array}$$

Multiply 2 ones by 8. Put 1 ten above the 5.

$$\begin{array}{r} \overset{4}{7}\,\overset{1}{5}\,2 \\ \times \quad 8 \\ \hline 16 \end{array}$$

Multiply 5 tens by 8. Then, add 1 ten. Put 4 hundreds above the 7.

$$\begin{array}{r} \overset{4}{7}\,\overset{1}{5}\,2 \\ \times \quad 8 \\ \hline 6016 \end{array}$$

Multiply 7 hundreds by 8. Then, add 4 hundreds.

Multiply.

	a	b	c	d	e	f
1.	118 × 3	305 × 4	224 × 5	152 × 3	200 × 7	137 × 5
2.	327 × 3	158 × 3	235 × 6	142 × 9	580 × 3	129 × 9
3.	335 × 5	190 × 7	421 × 8	201 × 9	287 × 3	243 × 4
4.	405 × 5	118 × 8	402 × 3	498 × 6	700 × 7	398 × 2
5.	652 × 3	142 × 4	704 × 8	193 × 7	246 × 3	152 × 7
6.	704 × 6	751 × 3	200 × 7	555 × 2	909 × 2	730 × 7

NAME ____________________

Lesson 4.7 Multiplying 2 Digits by 2 Digits

$$\begin{array}{r} 19 \\ \times 27 \\ \hline \end{array}$$

$$\begin{array}{r} {}^{6} \\ 19 \\ \times 27 \\ \hline 133 \end{array}$$

Multiply 9 ones by 7.
Put 6 tens above the 1.
Multiply 1 ten by 7.
Then, add 6 tens.

$$\begin{array}{r} {}^{1} \\ 19 \\ \times 27 \\ \hline 133 \\ 380 \end{array}$$

Multiply 9 ones by 20.
Put 1 ten above the 1.
Multiply 1 ten by 20.
Then, add 1 ten.

$$\begin{array}{r} 19 \\ \times 27 \\ \hline 133 \\ +380 \\ \hline 513 \end{array}$$ } Add.

Multiply.

	a	b	c	d	e	f
1.	22×33	11×45	80×10	31×23	13×12	30×31
2.	41×21	32×20	40×10	21×31	30×30	14×10
3.	22×44	14×20	40×12	90×10	13×13	30×11
4.	70×11	12×11	81×10	24×12	40×22	31×31

NAME ______________________

Lesson 4.8 Multiplying 2 Digits by 2 Digits (renaming)

Multiply.

	a	b	c	d	e	f
1.	22 × 19	32 × 41	72 × 18	45 × 15	48 × 20	77 × 22
2.	63 × 24	52 × 48	28 × 25	77 × 30	33 × 29	90 × 70
3.	57 × 23	18 × 18	77 × 27	65 × 17	88 × 22	90 × 20
4.	37 × 23	91 × 38	44 × 43	17 × 13	88 × 17	55 × 38

NAME ______________________

Lesson 4.9 Multiplying 3 Digits by 2 Digits (renaming)

Multiply.

	a	b	c	d	e	f
1.	315 × 30	527 × 42	287 × 21	242 × 70	209 × 30	813 × 17
2.	140 × 32	196 × 23	673 × 92	542 × 48	604 × 40	150 × 45
3.	713 × 67	900 × 42	198 × 72	513 × 58	841 × 71	379 × 84
4.	125 × 73	706 × 31	448 × 33	809 × 12	615 × 73	458 × 83

NAME ______________________

Lesson 4.10 Multiplying 4 Digits by 1 Digit (renaming)

$\begin{array}{r} \overset{2}{8{,}208} \\ \times \quad 3 \\ \hline 4 \end{array}$	Multiply 8 ones by 3. Put 2 tens above the 0.	$\begin{array}{r} \overset{2}{8{,}208} \\ \times \quad 3 \\ \hline 24 \end{array}$	Multiply 0 tens by 3. Then, add 2 tens.
$\begin{array}{r} \overset{2}{8{,}208} \\ \times \quad 3 \\ \hline 624 \end{array}$	Multiply 2 hundreds by 3.	$\begin{array}{r} \overset{2}{8{,}208} \\ \times \quad 3 \\ \hline 24{,}624 \end{array}$	Multiply 8 thousands by 3.

Multiply.

	a	b	c	d	e	f
1.	4,393 × 7	4,755 × 7	7,096 × 5	2,632 × 4	3,054 × 2	5,321 × 5
2.	9,443 × 2	6,356 × 5	7,553 × 3	5,448 × 1	4,321 × 7	1,496 × 9
3.	5,418 × 3	1,010 × 5	5,166 × 6	2,209 × 5	1,405 × 8	3,630 × 8
4.	2,887 × 1	3,117 × 8	8,412 × 1	6,348 × 3	2,341 × 4	8,115 × 6
5.	8,108 × 4	1,564 × 4	5,084 × 4	8,564 × 6	2,050 × 8	3,421 × 6
6.	8,402 × 4	1,763 × 8	9,536 × 5	2,910 × 9	6,478 × 2	5,467 × 1

NAME ___________________________

Lesson 4.11 Problem Solving

SHOW YOUR WORK

Solve each problem.

1. Xavier loves to eat pears. He ate 2 a day for 48 days. How many pears did Xavier eat?

   Xavier ate __________ pears.

2. Clayton keeps pet mice. If his 33 mice have 12 babies each, how many mice will Clayton have in all?

   Clayton will have __________ mice.

3. In a tropical rain forest, the average annual rainfall is about 150 inches. After 5 years, about how much rain will have fallen in the rain forest?

   About __________ inches of rain will have fallen.

4. A school of 2,368 students went on a field trip to collect seashells. If the students collected 3 shells each, how many shells did they collect?

   The students collected __________ shells.

5. Buses were reserved for the big field trip. If each bus holds 20 students, how many students would 6 buses hold?

   The buses would hold __________ students.

6. If 16 potato chips is a serving size and there are 5 servings per bag, how many potato chips are in each bag?

   There are __________ chips in a bag.

1.

2.

3.

4.

5.

6.

NAME ____________________

Check What You Learned

Multiplication

Multiply.

	a	b	c	d	e	f	g
1.	72 × 4	24 × 8	339 × 2	34 × 8	150 × 9	333 × 2	93 × 2
2.	242 × 2	64 × 8	31 × 7	300 × 21	7 × 9	173 × 28	90 × 8
3.	3,417 × 7	728 × 1	22 × 3	207 × 21	900 × 6	79 × 4	643 × 7
4.	743 × 2	439 × 10	117 × 23	943 × 6	2,981 × 6	200 × 9	555 × 40

List the factors of each number. Then, label each number as *prime* or *composite.*

		Factors	Prime or Composite?
5.	85	____________	____________
6.	59	____________	____________
7.	15	____________	____________
8.	26	____________	____________

NAME ______________________

Check What You Learned

SHOW YOUR WORK

Multiplication

Solve each problem.

9. Mrs. Rockwell checked on how much time her students spend doing homework. If all 23 students spend 20 hours a week, how much homework do the students do in a week?

They do __________ hours of homework a week.

10. A cable program loans channel boxes to 21 community centers for a trial program. If there are 12 boxes for each center, how many boxes are being loaned?

There are __________ boxes being loaned.

11. A girls' club is trying to get into the record books for the most hair braids. There are 372 girls. If each girl braids her hair into 40 little braids, how many braids will they have?

They will have __________ braids.

9.
10.
11.

Write the equation. Then, solve the problem.

12. Mrs. Numkena's science class raised tadpoles. If 35 students raised 23 tadpoles each, how many tadpoles did the class have?

_____ × _____ = _____

The class had __________ tadpoles.

13. At Lakeside View, 15 apartment houses were built. If there are 12 units to each apartment house, how many units are available?

_____ × _____ = _____

There are __________ units available.

12.
13.

CHAPTER 4 POSTTEST

NAME ______________________

Check What You Know

Division

Divide.

	a	b	c	d	e
1.	3)15	7)49	9)27	5)45	7)21
2.	3)18	7)42	9)81	7)56	3)30
3.	4)36	4)16	4)46	2)10	6)36
4.	9)18	5)35	7)28	2)6	4)24
5.	9)87	7)77	2)50	2)175	3)900
6.	3)45	5)105	5)500	8)78	3)68
7.	5)2,214	6)121	7)62	7)22	5)4,693

Check What You Know

Division

SHOW YOUR WORK

Solve each problem.

8. Lori found 42 shells at the beach. She gave the same number of shells to 7 of her friends. How many shells did she give to each friend?

She gave __________ shells to each friend.

9. The drama club is giving a party in the school lunchroom. The club wants to be seated in groups of 8. If 64 students go to the party, how many groups of students will there be?

There will be __________ groups of students.

10. The Pancake Restaurant served 32 pancakes. If 8 customers ate an equal number of pancakes, how many did each person eat?

Each person ate __________ pancakes.

11. The school spirit club baked cakes for a charity event. There were 75 different cakes and 5 bakers. Each baker baked the same number of cakes. How many cakes did each baker make?

Each baker made __________ cakes.

12. The Fish Shop is open 72 hours a week. The shop is open 6 days a week and the same number of hours each day. How many hours each day is the shop open?

The shop is open __________ hours a day.

13. The glee club needs to sell 382 tickets to win a trip. If there are 8 members who want to go on the trip, how many tickets does each member need to sell? How many extra tickets are left?

Each member needs to sell __________ tickets.

There will be __________ extra tickets.

8.

9.

10.

11.

12.

13.

NAME ______________________

Lesson 5.1 Dividing Multiples of 10 and 100

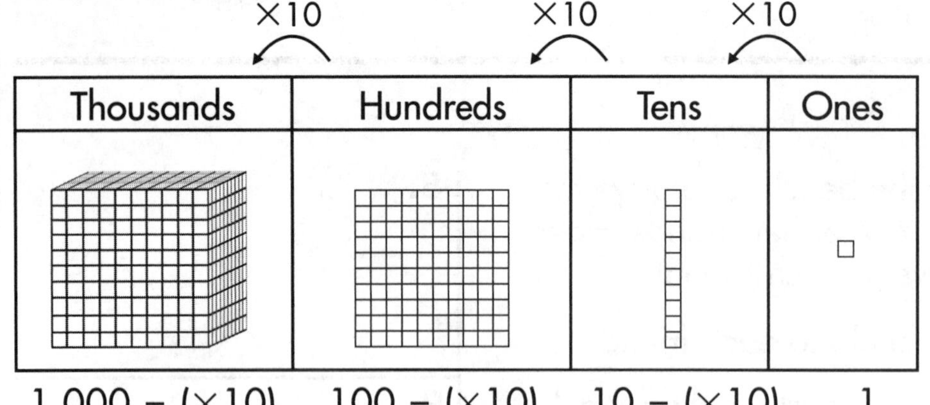

Division is the opposite of multiplication.

700 ÷ 70 = 10

Divide.

	a	b	c	d
1.	300 ÷ 3 =	60 ÷ 6 =	100 ÷ 10 =	20 ÷ 10 =
2.	800 ÷ 80 =	700 ÷ 10 =	4,000 ÷ 400 =	50 ÷ 10 =
3.	3,000 ÷ 10 =	400 ÷ 40 =	1,000 ÷ 10 =	80 ÷ 8 =
4.	600 ÷ 10 =	70 ÷ 7 =	9,000 ÷ 900 =	500 ÷ 10 =
5.	40 ÷ 10 =	7,000 ÷ 700 =	200 ÷ 10 =	90 ÷ 10 =

NAME ____________________

Lesson 5.2 Dividing through 45 ÷ 5

divisor → 7)22 ← dividend, with 9 ← quotient

To check your answer, do the inverse operation.

If 45 ÷ 5 = 9, then 5 × 9 = 45 must be true.

Using the division table, find 45 in the 5 column. The quotient is named at the beginning of the row.

5-column ↓ (divisors)

(quotients) — quotient →

x	0	1	2	3	4	5	6	7	8	9
0	0	0	0	0	0	0	0	0	0	0
1	0	1	2	3	4	5	6	7	8	9
2	0	2	4	6	8	10	12	14	16	18
3	0	3	6	9	12	15	18	21	24	27
4	0	4	8	12	16	20	24	28	32	36
5	0	5	10	15	20	25	30	35	40	45
6	0	6	12	18	24	30	36	42	48	54
7	0	7	14	21	28	35	42	49	56	63
8	0	8	16	24	32	40	48	56	64	72
9	0	9	18	27	36	45	54	63	72	81

Divide.

	a	b	c	d	e	f
1.	5)35	4)16	4)36	3)18	5)25	4)28
2.	2)18	3)18	3)27	3)12	5)20	3)21
3.	5)45	3)15	5)30	4)32	2)8	2)10
4.	2)16	2)12	9)45	5)35	2)18	5)40
5.	5)30	4)24	3)24	4)20	3)9	4)12
6.	2)14	4)4	5)15	5)10	4)0	3)6

Complete the following.

	a	b	c	d
7.	5 × 3 = 15 so 3)15	4 × 7 = 28 so 7)28	3 × 4 = 12 so 4)12	9 × 2 = 18 so 2)18

NAME ____________________

Lesson 5.3 Dividing through 63 ÷ 7

divisor → 7)63 ← dividend, with the quotient 9 written above ← quotient

$$7\overline{)63}$$

To check your answer, do the inverse operation.

If 63 ÷ 7 = 9, then 7 × 9 = 63 must be true.

Using the division table, find 63 in the 7 column. The quotient is named at the beginning of the row.

7-column

quotient

×	0	1	2	3	4	5	6	7	8	9
0	0	0	0	0	0	0	0	0	0	0
1	0	1	2	3	4	5	6	7	8	9
2	0	2	4	6	8	10	12	14	16	18
3	0	3	6	9	12	15	18	21	24	27
4	0	4	8	12	16	20	24	28	32	36
5	0	5	10	15	20	25	30	35	40	45
6	0	6	12	18	24	30	36	42	48	54
7	0	7	14	21	28	35	42	49	56	63
8	0	8	16	24	32	40	48	56	64	72
9	0	9	18	27	36	45	54	63	72	81

Divide.

	a	b	c	d	e	f
1.	7)49	5)45	6)36	3)24	3)27	4)28
2.	2)18	4)24	6)48	4)32	5)45	2)16
3.	5)40	2)12	6)6	7)56	7)0	6)54
4.	5)25	5)10	7)21	7)28	6)42	7)63
5.	6)24	4)20	7)35	5)30	4)12	4)16
6.	7)7	5)15	7)42	3)21	6)12	6)30

Complete the following.

7.

a. $7 \times 6 = 42$ so 6)42

b. $4 \times 6 = 24$ so 6)24

c. $8 \times 7 = 56$ so 7)56

NAME ____________________

Lesson 5.4 Dividing through 81 ÷ 9

$$\begin{array}{r} 9 \\ 9\overline{)81} \end{array}$$

divisor → 9; 9 ← quotient; 81 ← dividend

To check your answer, do the inverse operation.

If 81 ÷ 9 = 9, then 9 × 9 = 81 must be true.

Using the division table, find 81 in the 9 column. The quotient is named at the beginning of the row.

9-column

x	0	1	2	3	4	5	6	7	8	9
0	0	0	0	0	0	0	0	0	0	0
1	0	1	2	3	4	5	6	7	8	9
2	0	2	4	6	8	10	12	14	16	18
3	0	3	6	9	12	15	18	21	24	27
4	0	4	8	12	16	20	24	28	32	36
5	0	5	10	15	20	25	30	35	40	45
6	0	6	12	18	24	30	36	42	48	54
7	0	7	14	21	28	35	42	49	56	63
8	0	8	16	24	32	40	48	56	64	72
9	0	9	18	27	36	45	54	63	72	81

quotient →

Divide.

	a	b	c	d	e	f
1.	$9\overline{)72}$	$8\overline{)40}$	$8\overline{)24}$	$6\overline{)48}$	$7\overline{)28}$	$6\overline{)36}$
2.	$6\overline{)18}$	$3\overline{)21}$	$7\overline{)49}$	$9\overline{)54}$	$9\overline{)81}$	$4\overline{)32}$
3.	$5\overline{)35}$	$7\overline{)56}$	$9\overline{)18}$	$7\overline{)42}$	$9\overline{)36}$	$7\overline{)28}$
4.	$9\overline{)45}$	$5\overline{)30}$	$4\overline{)12}$	$5\overline{)25}$	$7\overline{)14}$	$9\overline{)0}$
5.	$9\overline{)9}$	$8\overline{)40}$	$8\overline{)48}$	$6\overline{)42}$	$3\overline{)27}$	$4\overline{)28}$

Complete the following.

	a	b	c
6.	$\begin{array}{r} 7 \\ \times\ 5 \\ \hline 35 \end{array}$ so $5\overline{)35}$	$\begin{array}{r} 8 \\ \times\ 8 \\ \hline 64 \end{array}$ so $8\overline{)64}$	$\begin{array}{r} 9 \\ \times\ 6 \\ \hline 54 \end{array}$ so $6\overline{)54}$
7.	$\begin{array}{r} 9 \\ \times\ 4 \\ \hline 36 \end{array}$ so $4\overline{)36}$	$\begin{array}{r} 6 \\ \times\ 4 \\ \hline 24 \end{array}$ so $4\overline{)24}$	$\begin{array}{r} 6 \\ \times\ 8 \\ \hline 48 \end{array}$ so $8\overline{)48}$

NAME ____________________

Lesson 5.5 Division Practice

Divide.

	a	b	c	d	e
1.	$8\overline{)56}$	$6\overline{)24}$	$2\overline{)18}$	$5\overline{)35}$	$7\overline{)42}$
2.	$6\overline{)48}$	$6\overline{)30}$	$8\overline{)72}$	$6\overline{)36}$	$9\overline{)81}$
3.	$9\overline{)54}$	$3\overline{)21}$	$7\overline{)28}$	$3\overline{)18}$	$2\overline{)18}$
4.	$5\overline{)45}$	$9\overline{)36}$	$6\overline{)42}$	$8\overline{)64}$	$7\overline{)63}$
5.	$3\overline{)24}$	$9\overline{)27}$	$5\overline{)20}$	$7\overline{)49}$	$5\overline{)25}$
6.	$5\overline{)40}$	$7\overline{)14}$	$9\overline{)81}$	$9\overline{)0}$	$4\overline{)16}$

NAME ____________________

Lesson 5.6 Problem Solving

SHOW YOUR WORK

Solve each problem.

1. Eddie and Toru listened to 72 of their favorite songs. If there were 9 songs on each album, how many albums did they listen to?

   They listened to ________ albums.

2. Mr. Luiz printed 35 tests for his students. If there were 7 rows of students, how many tests were passed out to each row?

   There were ________ tests passed out to each row.

3. Gary opened a bag of candy containing 81 pieces. He wants to give each of his guests the same number of pieces. If he has 9 guests, how many pieces does each person get?

   Each guest gets ________ pieces.

4. Last year, Mrs. Ford decided to give chores to each person in the family. Each person got the same number of chores. There are 8 family members. If there were 32 chores, how many did each person get?

   Each person got ________ chores.

5. It takes 16 hours to drive to the dunes. Tasha and her brother Kurt will drive the same number of hours. How many hours will each of them drive?

   Each of them will drive ________ hours.

6. The Pet Warehouse received 63 boxes of cat litter. The same number of boxes will be sent to 9 stores. How many boxes will each store get?

   Each store will get ________ boxes.

1.
2.
3.
4.
5.
6.

NAME ____________________

Lesson 5.7 Dividing 2 Digits

×	1	2	3	4	5
8	8	16	24	32	40

$$\begin{array}{r} 4 \\ 8\overline{)33} \\ -32 \\ \hline 1 \end{array}$$

8 × 4 — Subtract.

33 is between 32 and 40, so 33 ÷ 8 is between 4 and 5. The ones digit is 4.

Since 33 − 32 = 1 and 1 is less than 8, the remainder 1 is recorded like this:

$$\begin{array}{r} 4 \text{ r}1 \\ 8\overline{)33} \\ -32 \\ \hline 1 \end{array}$$

Divide.

	a	b	c	d	e
1.	$5\overline{)26}$	$7\overline{)58}$	$4\overline{)31}$	$9\overline{)82}$	$6\overline{)35}$
2.	$8\overline{)66}$	$3\overline{)17}$	$2\overline{)13}$	$7\overline{)50}$	$6\overline{)40}$
3.	$9\overline{)30}$	$5\overline{)41}$	$3\overline{)10}$	$8\overline{)73}$	$7\overline{)57}$
4.	$8\overline{)20}$	$6\overline{)37}$	$9\overline{)55}$	$7\overline{)29}$	$5\overline{)47}$

NAME ______________________________

Lesson 5.7 Dividing 2 Digits

×	10	20	30
3	30	60	90

$$\begin{array}{r} 2 \\ 3\overline{)67} \\ -60 \\ \hline 7 \end{array}$$

3 × 20 — -60

Subtract. — 7

67 is between 60 and 90, so 67 ÷ 3 is between 20 and 30. The tens digit is 2.

×	1	2	3
3	3	6	9

$$\begin{array}{r} 22 \text{ r}1 \\ 3\overline{)67} \\ -60 \\ \hline 7 \\ -6 \\ \hline 1 \end{array}$$

3 × 2 = 6, so the ones digit is 2.

3 × 2 = 6

Subtract.

remainder

Divide.

	a	b	c	d	e
1.	$2\overline{)36}$	$5\overline{)76}$	$7\overline{)79}$	$4\overline{)96}$	$7\overline{)93}$
2.	$5\overline{)86}$	$3\overline{)96}$	$8\overline{)99}$	$7\overline{)84}$	$3\overline{)75}$
3.	$6\overline{)93}$	$6\overline{)73}$	$8\overline{)89}$	$7\overline{)89}$	$9\overline{)99}$
4.	$4\overline{)88}$	$3\overline{)84}$	$2\overline{)77}$	$4\overline{)78}$	$8\overline{)93}$

NAME ______________________________

Lesson 5.8 Dividing 3 Digits

Since $100 \times 8 = 800$ and 800 is greater than 453, there is no hundreds digit.

$8\overline{)453}$

×	10	20	30	40	50	60
8	80	160	240	320	400	480

453 is between 400 and 480. $453 \div 8$ is between 50 and 60. The tens digit is 5.

```
   5
8)453
 - 40     8 × 5 = 40
   53     Subtract.
```

×	1	2	3	4	5	6	7
8	8	16	24	32	40	48	56

53 is between 48 and 56. $53 \div 8$ is between 6 and 7. The ones digit is 6.

```
   5 r5
8)453
 - 40
   53     8 × 6 = 48
   48     Subtract.
    5     remainder
```

Divide.

	a	b	c	d	e
1.	$8\overline{)720}$	$4\overline{)327}$	$9\overline{)372}$	$4\overline{)173}$	$2\overline{)150}$
2.	$6\overline{)552}$	$3\overline{)139}$	$4\overline{)248}$	$9\overline{)890}$	$5\overline{)105}$
3.	$9\overline{)780}$	$5\overline{)225}$	$9\overline{)813}$	$7\overline{)511}$	$3\overline{)110}$

NAME ______________________________

Lesson 5.8 Dividing 3 Digits

Divide.

	a	b	c	d	e
1.	$6\overline{)773}$	$2\overline{)898}$	$4\overline{)566}$	$6\overline{)781}$	$3\overline{)972}$
2.	$2\overline{)317}$	$4\overline{)732}$	$9\overline{)989}$	$7\overline{)897}$	$2\overline{)394}$
3.	$5\overline{)529}$	$8\overline{)897}$	$3\overline{)676}$	$2\overline{)348}$	$6\overline{)930}$
4.	$3\overline{)784}$	$5\overline{)788}$	$3\overline{)481}$	$5\overline{)558}$	$2\overline{)610}$
5.	$3\overline{)324}$	$5\overline{)953}$	$4\overline{)868}$	$3\overline{)975}$	$6\overline{)720}$

NAME ______________________

Lesson 5.9 Dividing 4 Digits

$8 \div 4 = 2$ $4 \times 2 = 8$	$9 \div 4 = 2$ remainder 1	$11 \div 4 = 2$ remainder 3	$37 \div 4 = 9$ remainder 1
$4\overline{)8917}$ quotient 2 −8 09	$4\overline{)8917}$ quotient 22 −8 09 −8 11	$4\overline{)8917}$ quotient 222 −8 09 −8 11 −8 37	$4\overline{)8917}$ quotient 222 −8 09 −8 11 −8 37 −36 1

divisor (4) — dividend (8917) — quotient (222) — remainder (1)

Divide.

	a	b	c	d	e
1.	$2\overline{)2,612}$	$5\overline{)8,603}$	$4\overline{)8,263}$	$3\overline{)6,363}$	$7\overline{)6,137}$
2.	$6\overline{)6,219}$	$2\overline{)4,921}$	$8\overline{)9,061}$	$9\overline{)1,616}$	$3\overline{)8,813}$
3.	$2\overline{)3,164}$	$5\overline{)8,373}$	$7\overline{)3,029}$	$4\overline{)7,176}$	$3\overline{)1,256}$

NAME ______________________

Lesson 5.9 Dividing 4 Digits

$21 \div 6 = 3$ remainder 3

$$\begin{array}{r} 3 \\ 6\overline{)2142} \\ -18 \\ \hline 34 \end{array}$$

$34 \div 6 = 5$ remainder 4

$$\begin{array}{r} 35 \\ 6\overline{)2142} \\ -18 \\ \hline 34 \\ -30 \\ \hline 42 \end{array}$$

$42 \div 6 = 7$

$$\begin{array}{r} 357 \\ 6\overline{)2142} \\ -18 \\ \hline 34 \\ -30 \\ \hline 42 \\ -42 \\ \hline 0 \end{array}$$

Divide.

	a	b	c	d	e
1.	$4\overline{)4,783}$	$4\overline{)1,207}$	$5\overline{)3,901}$	$2\overline{)9,131}$	$5\overline{)3,197}$
2.	$2\overline{)6,641}$	$7\overline{)3,440}$	$5\overline{)5,517}$	$8\overline{)4,304}$	$3\overline{)6,365}$
3.	$3\overline{)8,421}$	$1\overline{)7,412}$	$2\overline{)2,258}$	$1\overline{)7,293}$	$2\overline{)8,473}$

NAME ____________________

Lesson 5.10 Problem Solving

SHOW YOUR WORK

Solve each problem.

1. Ms. Garrett had 40 guests at her birthday party. She cut her cake into 88 slices. Each guest ate 2 pieces of cake. How many slices were left?

   There were ________ slices left.

2. Lucy babysits for 2 families. She works the same number of hours each month for each family. If she worked 76 hours last month, how many hours did she work for each family?

   She worked ________ hours for each family.

3. The garden show is moving into a bigger area. The new space has 935 square feet of space for displays. There are 16 different displays, and each display will need the same amount of space. How many square feet does each display get? How many square feet are left over?

   Each display gets ________ square feet of space.

   There are ________ square feet of space left over.

4. A boys' club picked up litter in the park. They collected 913 bags of litter. If each boy collected about the same amount, about how many bags did the 7 boys collect? How many extra bags were collected?

   Each boy picked up about ________ bags.

   There were ________ extra bags collected.

5. The school supply store received a shipment of 3,650 pens. If the pens are packed in 5 boxes, how many pens are in each box?

   There are ________ pens in each box.

1.

2.

3.

4.

5.

NAME ____________________

Check What You Learned

Division

Divide.

	a	b	c	d	e
1.	3)18	9)27	7)7	8)64	4)40
2.	9)72	6)36	8)16	7)21	4)28
3.	5)25	8)64	9)54	5)35	3)12
4.	7)49	9)9	7)21	2)18	3)18
5.	2)96	3)87	8)93	30)300	7)31
6.	8)75	2)19	8)43	9)89	3)66
7.	3)6,118	5)917	6)762	7)37	2)48

CHAPTER 5 POSTTEST

NAME ____________________

Check What You Learned

Division

SHOW YOUR WORK

Solve each problem.

8. A group of 7 boys cut lawns over the weekend. They made 56 dollars. Each boy will make the same amount. How much money will each boy get? Each boy will get ________ dollars.	**8.**
9. Gloria decided to make lemonade for her family. There are 8 people in her family. The pitcher will hold 24 glasses of lemonade. How many glasses can each person have? Each person can have ________ glasses.	**9.**
10. Susan, Marta, and Aisha have 5 hours to spend at the zoo. There are 40 different animals they want to see. During each hour at the zoo, how many animals should they plan to see? They should plan to see ________ different animals each hour.	**10.**
11. At baseball practice, 325 pitches were thrown to the players. If 5 players got the same number of pitches, how many pitches did each player get? Each player got ________ pitches.	**11.**
12. Taylor needs 612 more dollars to buy a plane ticket to visit his cousin in Australia. If he saves 9 dollars a day, how soon can he go to Australia? He will have the rest of the money in _____ days.	**12.**
13. The bait shop ordered 136 fishing worms for their customers. The workers put them into 8 separate cups. How many worms are in each cup? There are ________ worms in each cup.	**13.**

NAME ______________________________

Mid-Test Chapters 1–5

Add or subtract.

	a	b	c	d	e
1.	23 + 2	33 + 6	17 + 2	32 + 7	61 + 5
2.	14 + 5	73 + 1	80 + 9	52 + 7	71 + 8
3.	23 + 7	82 + 9	74 + 7	31 + 9	33 + 8
4.	38 + 5	57 + 8	86 + 8	72 + 9	24 + 9
5.	32 − 1	86 − 14	25 − 15	87 − 34	97 − 65
6.	74 − 8	93 − 9	17 − 8	63 − 8	38 − 19
7.	52 + 17	32 + 17 + 10	37 + 25	43 + 21 + 18	73 + 26
8.	36 + 13	75 + 18	41 + 39	57 + 18	37 + 28
9.	320 − 18	715 − 23	287 − 78	555 − 98	408 − 19
10.	973 − 84	578 − 99	300 − 17	542 − 80	663 − 74

NAME ______________________

Mid-Test Chapters 1–5

Write each number in expanded form.

	a	b	c
11.	732	32,132	4,790
12.	1,003	2,314,732	3,001

Round each number to the place named.

	a	b	c
13.	13,573 hundreds	75,319 ten thousands	1,932,710 millions
14.	4,935 tens	357,013 hundred thousands	4,015 tens

Compare each pair of numbers. Write >, <, or =.

	a	b	c
15.	13,702 ___ 13,207	3,976 ___ 9,362	932 ___ nine hundred one
16.	26,314 ___ 260,314	978 ___ 978	3,721,460 ___ 3,710,460

Add.

	a	b	c	d	e
17.	703 +172	665 +118	713 +375	511 +430	300 +479
18.	2314 + 718	1725 + 625	3201 +1405	7358 +1757	8101 +1709

CHAPTERS 1–5 MID-TEST

NAME ____________________

Mid-Test Chapters 1–5

Subtract.

	a	b	c	d	e
19.	32146 − 3132	67315 −14305	40195 − 9186	75532 −21530	25789 − 6642
20.	17315 − 8904	98789 −73979	42804 −38709	87897 −58898	34932 −17983
21.	32564 − 2198	4397 −2810	39702 − 615	32084 −18093	9327 − 452

Add.

	a	b	c	d	e
22.	4132 714 + 304	32015 + 7932	8215 1730 +1045	25713 +13846	3014 1246 + 710
23.	83548 + 8162	2315 1215 720 + 214	37805 +12125	7300 715 243 + 120	71042 + 8925
24.	5614 +3293	26417 + 2815	4932 + 512	108765 + 2046	45059 +38712

CHAPTERS 1–5 MID-TEST

NAME ____________________

Mid-Test Chapters 1–5

Multiply.

	a	b	c	d	e
25.	7×8	9×4	7×4	8×6	21×4
26.	32×3	14×2	44×2	12×4	20×4
27.	32×7	47×3	21×8	40×9	17×9
28.	48×7	72×8	84×4	25 7	49×9

	a	b	c	d	e	f
29.	11×10	22×11	31×32	43×20	50×10	31×20
30.	75×25	32×18	132×41	81×37	103×17	282×38
31.	418×45	500×32	199×47	578×23	887×52	399×19

CHAPTERS 1–5 MID-TEST

NAME ______________________________

Mid-Test Chapters 1–5

Divide.

	a	b	c	d	e
32.	$9\overline{)81}$	$7\overline{)56}$	$8\overline{)48}$	$8\overline{)64}$	$7\overline{)42}$
33.	$8\overline{)24}$	$5\overline{)35}$	$7\overline{)28}$	$6\overline{)54}$	$9\overline{)90}$
34.	$3\overline{)300}$	$2\overline{)642}$	$7\overline{)721}$	$4\overline{)484}$	$8\overline{)864}$
35.	$8\overline{)724}$	$7\overline{)639}$	$5\overline{)525}$	$6\overline{)247}$	$2\overline{)876}$
36.	$9\overline{)458}$	$7\overline{)8,207}$	$6\overline{)684}$	$3\overline{)949}$	$4\overline{)713}$
37.	$9\overline{)908}$	$2\overline{)510}$	$4\overline{)6,481}$	$8\overline{)888}$	$6\overline{)445}$

Mid-Test Chapters 1–5

SHOW YOUR WORK

Solve each problem.

38. A total of 68 hikers went on a trip to Blue Hill Mountain. If 32 of the hikers were boys, how many hikers were girls?

__________ hikers were girls.

39. On a trip to Washington, DC, there were 33 fifth-graders and 27 fourth-graders. How many students were on the trip?

There were __________ students on the trip.

40. At the picnic grove, bird watchers saw 42 robins looking for worms. If there were 5 times as many starlings as robins, how many starlings were there?

There were __________ starlings.

41. A group of friends is getting ready for a hike at night. Each of their flashlights take 4 batteries. If they have 72 batteries, how many flashlights can they take?

They can take __________ flashlights.

42. There are 21 members of the soccer team on the bus. If each player carries on 4 pieces of equipment, how many pieces of equipment are on the bus?

There are __________ pieces of equipment on the bus.

43. At the high school, all textbooks must be turned in at the end of the year. There are 150 science books, 125 math books, and 107 Spanish books. How many books will be turned in?

__________ books will be turned in.

38.

39.

40.

41.

42.

43.

NAME ______________________

Check What You Know

Fractions

To find an equivalent fraction, multiply the fraction by the number in the circle.

	a	b	c	d
1.	$\frac{3}{6}$ = ____ ④	$\frac{2}{3}$ = ____ ⑤	$\frac{1}{6}$ = ____ ⑥	$\frac{1}{3}$ = ____ ⑨

Draw a picture to compare the fractions. Then, write >, <, or =.

2. $\frac{1}{5}$ ○ $\frac{2}{10}$

Add.

3. $\frac{7}{10} + \frac{3}{10}$

4. $\frac{3}{8} + \frac{4}{8}$

Subtract.

5. $\frac{4}{5} - \frac{2}{5}$

6. $\frac{11}{12} - \frac{8}{12} =$

Decompose the fraction.

7. $\frac{2}{4}$

Write the decimal and fraction for each model.

8. 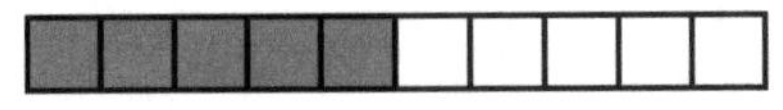

____ or ____

9. 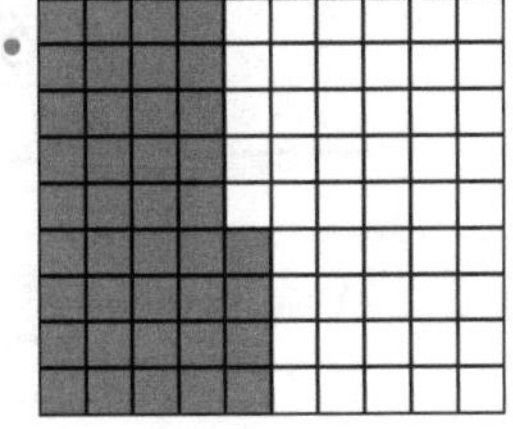

____ or ____

10. 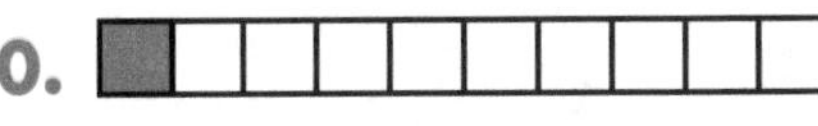

____ or ____

NAME ______________________

Check What You Know

Fractions

Add or subtract.

	a	b	c	d
11.	$\frac{4}{10} + \frac{8}{100}$	$7\frac{1}{6} + 3\frac{1}{6}$	$5\frac{3}{8} + 8\frac{3}{8}$	$8\frac{3}{5} + 8\frac{1}{5}$
12.	$7\frac{7}{9} - 4\frac{4}{9}$	$\frac{2}{10} + \frac{2}{100}$	$9\frac{3}{10} + 2\frac{9}{10}$	$4\frac{5}{7} - 1\frac{2}{7}$

Multiply.

	a	b	c	d
13.	$\frac{8}{9} \times 4 =$ ____	$3 \times \frac{1}{8} =$ ____	$\frac{4}{7} \times 2 =$ ____	$\frac{5}{7} \times 8 =$ ____
14.	$5 \times \frac{3}{10} =$ ____	$2 \times \frac{7}{12} =$ ____	$\frac{6}{11} \times 7 =$ ____	$\frac{2}{9} \times 8 =$ ____

NAME ____________________

Lesson 6.1 Finding Equivalent Fractions

$\frac{3}{4}$ To find an equivalent fraction, multiply both the numerator and denominator by the same number.

$\frac{3}{4} = \frac{3 \times 3}{4 \times 3} = \frac{9}{12}$ ⟵ Multiply the numerator by 3. ⟵ Multiply the denominator by 3.

$\frac{3}{4} = \frac{9}{12}$ $\frac{3}{4}$ and $\frac{9}{12}$ are equivalent fractions.

To find an equivalent fraction, multiply the fraction by the number in the circle.

	a	b	c	d
1.	$\frac{3}{4} =$ ____ ③	$\frac{1}{4} =$ ____ ④	$\frac{2}{3} =$ ____ ⑤	$\frac{1}{2} =$ ____ ②
2.	$\frac{1}{3} =$ ____ ⑥	$\frac{3}{12} =$ ____ ②	$\frac{1}{5} =$ ____ ③	$\frac{2}{10} =$ ____ ④
3.	$\frac{5}{7} =$ ____ ②	$\frac{3}{6} =$ ____ ④	$\frac{2}{8} =$ ____ ④	$\frac{1}{6} =$ ____ ⑥
4.	$\frac{1}{3} =$ ____ ⑨	$\frac{2}{3} =$ ____ ⑩	$\frac{2}{5} =$ ____ ⑤	$\frac{1}{8} =$ ____ ②

Use multiplication to find each equivalent fraction.

5.	$\frac{1}{5} = \frac{3}{\quad}$	$\frac{1}{10} = \frac{\quad}{20}$	$\frac{3}{4} = \frac{9}{\quad}$	$\frac{1}{2} = \frac{9}{\quad}$
6.	$\frac{1}{3} = \frac{\quad}{12}$	$\frac{2}{4} = \frac{8}{\quad}$	$\frac{1}{12} = \frac{2}{\quad}$	$\frac{2}{6} = \frac{\quad}{18}$
7.	$\frac{2}{8} = \frac{10}{\quad}$	$\frac{3}{5} = \frac{\quad}{25}$	$\frac{3}{7} = \frac{9}{\quad}$	$\frac{1}{2} = \frac{\quad}{20}$
8.	$\frac{4}{12} = \frac{\quad}{24}$	$\frac{5}{6} = \frac{\quad}{24}$	$\frac{1}{3} = \frac{9}{\quad}$	$\frac{1}{2} = \frac{\quad}{18}$

NAME ____________________

Lesson 6.2 Comparing Fractions Using Models

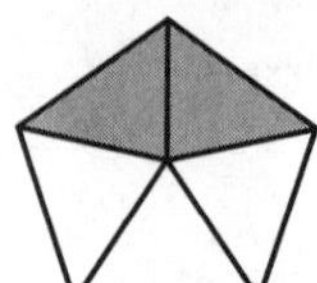
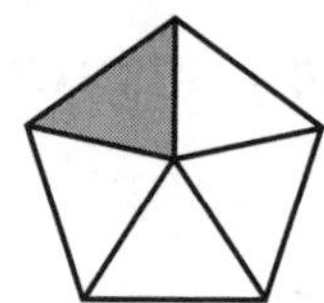
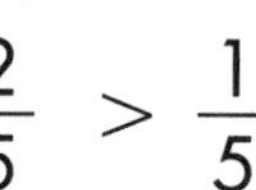

$\frac{2}{5} > \frac{1}{5}$

$\frac{2}{5}$ is greater than $\frac{1}{5}$.

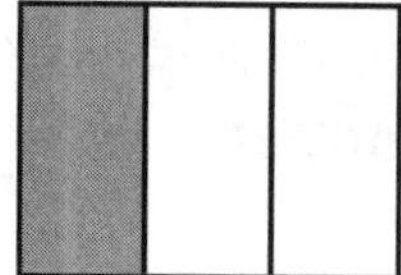
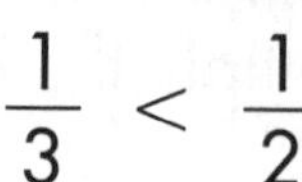

$\frac{1}{3} < \frac{1}{2}$

$\frac{1}{3}$ is less than $\frac{1}{2}$.

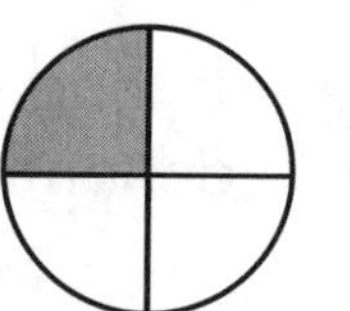
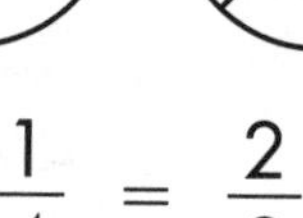

$\frac{1}{4} = \frac{2}{8}$

$\frac{1}{4}$ is equal to $\frac{2}{8}$.

Draw a picture for each fraction. Then, write <, >, or = to compare the fractions.

	a	b	c
1.	$\frac{1}{4}$ ○ $\frac{3}{4}$	$\frac{1}{2}$ ○ $\frac{2}{4}$ 	$\frac{2}{3}$ ○ $\frac{1}{2}$
2.	$\frac{7}{10}$ ○ $\frac{3}{5}$	$\frac{3}{8}$ ○ $\frac{3}{4}$ 	$\frac{1}{3}$ ○ $\frac{5}{8}$
3.	$\frac{1}{5}$ ○ $\frac{2}{10}$	$\frac{3}{4}$ ○ $\frac{1}{2}$ 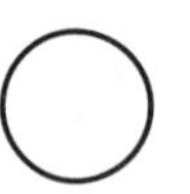	$\frac{6}{10}$ ○ $\frac{2}{5}$ 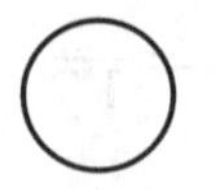

NAME ______________________________

Lesson 6.3 Comparing Fractions Using LCM

$\frac{1}{7} \bigcirc \frac{2}{3}$

$\frac{1 \times 3}{7 \times 3} = \frac{3}{21}$

$\frac{2 \times 3}{3 \times 3} = \frac{14}{21}$

$\frac{3}{21} < \frac{14}{21}$

To compare fractions without pictures, the denominators must be the same. When you have unlike denominators, find the **least common multiple (LCM)** and rename the fractions.
In the example, the denominators are 3 and 7, so find the LCM of 3 and 7.

Multiples of 3: 3, 6, 9, 12, 15, 18, (21), 24

Multiples of 7: 7, 14, (21), 28

The least common multiple of 3 and 7 is 21. To change each fraction so it has the same denominator, multiply both the numerator and denominator by the same number. Look at the numerator to determine the larger fraction.

Use <, >, or = to compare the fractions. Show your work.

	a	b
1.	$\frac{4}{8} \bigcirc \frac{2}{10}$	$\frac{1}{5} \bigcirc \frac{2}{10}$
2.	$\frac{3}{8} \bigcirc \frac{10}{12}$	$\frac{3}{12} \bigcirc \frac{1}{3}$
3.	$\frac{2}{8} \bigcirc \frac{1}{4}$	$\frac{3}{6} \bigcirc \frac{4}{8}$

NAME ______________________

Lesson 6.4 Adding Fractions with Like Denominators

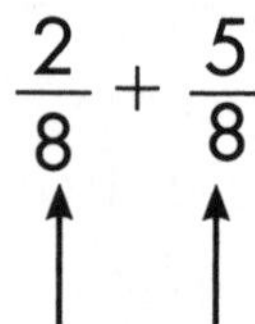

$\frac{2}{8} + \frac{5}{8}$

Like denominators are the same number.

Add the numerators.

$$\frac{2}{8} + \frac{5}{8} = \frac{2+5}{8} = \frac{7}{8}$$

Write the sum over the common denominator.

Add.

	a	b	c	d
1.	$\frac{3}{12} + \frac{8}{12} =$ ____	$\frac{2}{5} + \frac{1}{5} =$ ____	$\frac{3}{6} + \frac{2}{6} =$ ____	$\frac{1}{4} + \frac{2}{4} =$ ____
2.	$\frac{1}{10} + \frac{3}{10} =$ ____	$\frac{3}{8} + \frac{2}{8} =$ ____	$\frac{1}{3} + \frac{1}{3} =$ ____	$\frac{2}{7} + \frac{2}{7} =$ ____
3.	$\frac{3}{5} + \frac{1}{5} =$ ____	$\frac{4}{12} + \frac{5}{12} =$ ____	$\frac{3}{10} + \frac{6}{10} =$ ____	$\frac{2}{5} + \frac{2}{5} =$ ____

	a	b	c	d	e
4.	$\frac{3}{8} + \frac{2}{8}$	$\frac{3}{12} + \frac{4}{12}$	$\frac{1}{6} + \frac{1}{6}$	$\frac{2}{6} + \frac{1}{6}$	$\frac{1}{8} + \frac{1}{8}$
5.	$\frac{5}{12} + \frac{3}{12}$	$\frac{3}{7} + \frac{4}{7}$	$\frac{7}{10} + \frac{2}{10}$	$\frac{3}{5} + \frac{1}{5}$	$\frac{8}{12} + \frac{3}{12}$
6.	$\frac{5}{11} + \frac{3}{11}$	$\frac{1}{4} + \frac{1}{4}$	$\frac{1}{2} + \frac{1}{2}$	$\frac{5}{7} + \frac{1}{7}$	$\frac{3}{9} + \frac{1}{9}$

NAME ______________________________

Lesson 6.5 Subtracting Fractions with Like Denominators

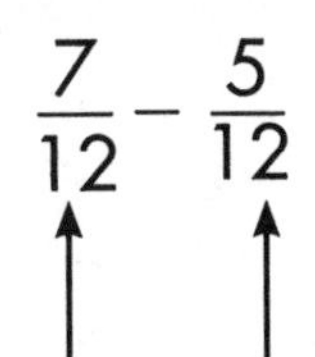

Like denominators are the same number.

Subtract the numerators.

$$\frac{7}{12} - \frac{5}{12} = \frac{7-5}{12} = \frac{2}{12}$$

Write the difference over the common denominator.

Subtract.

	a	b	c	d	e
1.	$\frac{11}{12} - \frac{3}{12}$	$\frac{7}{10} - \frac{3}{10}$	$\frac{3}{4} - \frac{1}{4}$	$\frac{6}{7} - \frac{5}{7}$	$\frac{4}{5} - \frac{3}{5}$
2.	$\frac{5}{10} - \frac{3}{10}$	$\frac{8}{12} - \frac{7}{12}$	$\frac{4}{5} - \frac{2}{5}$	$\frac{7}{10} - \frac{4}{10}$	$\frac{5}{8} - \frac{1}{8}$
3.	$\frac{9}{10} - \frac{3}{10}$	$\frac{7}{11} - \frac{5}{11}$	$\frac{8}{9} - \frac{1}{9}$	$\frac{4}{5} - \frac{2}{5}$	$\frac{8}{9} - \frac{6}{9}$

	a	b	c	d
4.	$\frac{5}{7} - \frac{3}{7} =$ ____	$\frac{7}{12} - \frac{3}{12} =$ ____	$\frac{8}{9} - \frac{8}{9} =$ ____	$\frac{12}{12} - \frac{8}{12} =$ ____
5.	$\frac{9}{12} - \frac{7}{12} =$ ____	$\frac{4}{4} - \frac{3}{4} =$ ____	$\frac{9}{10} - \frac{7}{10} =$ ____	$\frac{3}{3} - \frac{1}{3} =$ ____
6.	$\frac{5}{8} - \frac{1}{8} =$ ____	$\frac{6}{7} - \frac{5}{7} =$ ____	$\frac{11}{12} - \frac{8}{12} =$ ____	$\frac{7}{10} - \frac{0}{10} =$ ____

NAME ______________________

Lesson 6.6 Decomposing Fractions

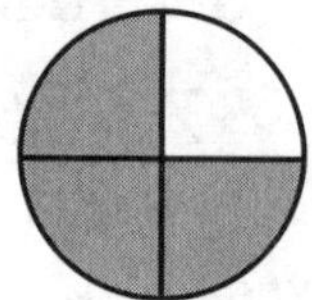
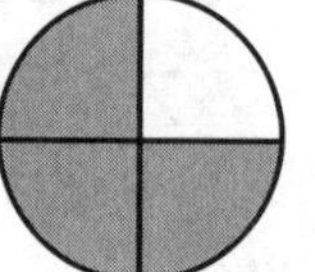

$\frac{3}{4}$

$\frac{1}{4} + \frac{1}{4} + \frac{1}{4} = \frac{3}{4}$

OR

$\frac{2}{4} + \frac{1}{4} = \frac{3}{4}$

Decompose each fraction in two ways. Write two equations to show your thinking.

	a	b
1.	$\frac{3}{5}$ 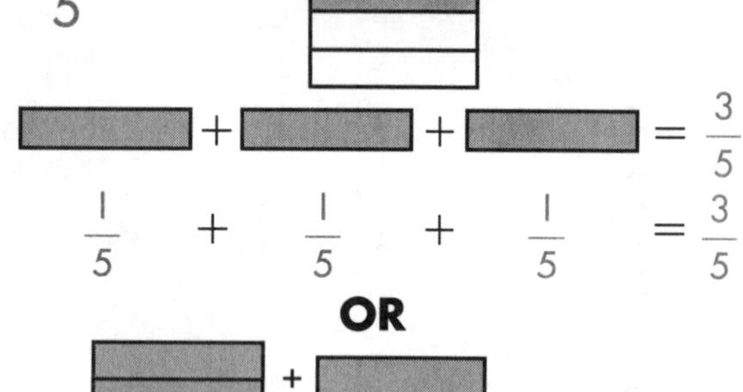 $\frac{1}{5} + \frac{1}{5} + \frac{1}{5} = \frac{3}{5}$ **OR** $\frac{2}{5} + \frac{1}{5} = \frac{3}{5}$	$\frac{5}{6}$
2.	$\frac{4}{12}$	$\frac{3}{8}$

NAME ____________________

Lesson 6.7 Problem Solving

SHOW YOUR WORK

Solve each problem. Show your work using fraction models.

1. Three sisters had to wash the family car. Paula washed the front $\frac{1}{3}$ and Kelley washed the back $\frac{1}{3}$ of the car. Mandy didn't show up to wash her part of the car. How much of the car was washed?

_____ of the car was washed.

2. Autumn has a bag of apples to feed her horses. If she feeds $\frac{2}{4}$ of the bag to her favorite horse and $\frac{1}{4}$ to the new foal, how much of the bag is left to feed the other horses?

_____ of a bag of apples is left for the other horses.

3. The library received $\frac{3}{5}$ of its book order. The next day, it received $\frac{1}{5}$ of the order. How much of the book order does the library have?

The library has _____ of the book order.

1.
2.
3.

Solve each problem. Show your work using equations.

4. A group of friends went to the movies. In the lobby, $\frac{4}{8}$ of the group decided to see a comedy and $\frac{2}{8}$ decided to see a mystery. How much of the group wanted to see either a comedy or a mystery?

_____ of the group wanted to see a comedy or a mystery.

5. In the school cafeteria, $\frac{2}{7}$ of the students were fourth-graders and $\frac{3}{7}$ of the students were fifth-graders. How many students were from the fourth and fifth grades?

_____ of the students were from the fourth and fifth grades.

4.
5.

NAME ___________________________

Lesson 6.8 Understanding Decimals to Tenths

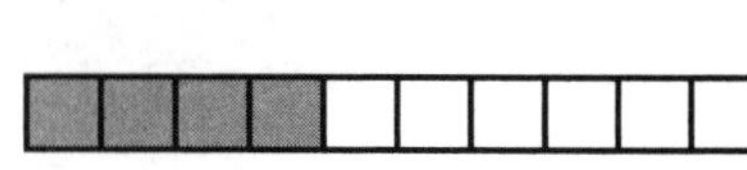

$\frac{4}{10}$ of the box is shaded. $\frac{4}{10}$ = four tenths = 0.4

$\frac{6}{10}$ of the box is unshaded. $\frac{6}{10}$ = six tenths = 0.6

Locate on a number line.

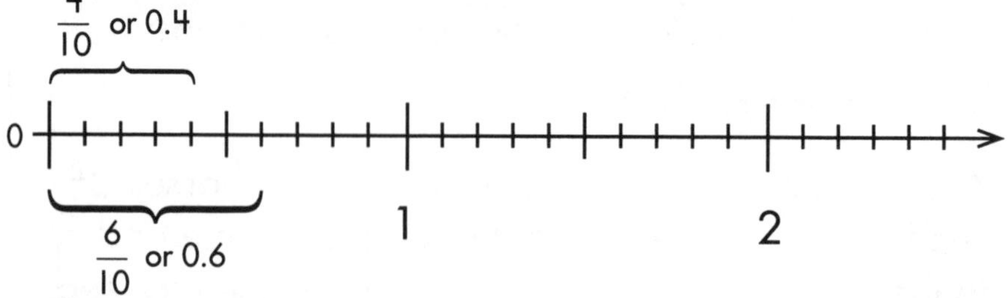

Write the decimal and fraction for each box.

	a	b	c
1.	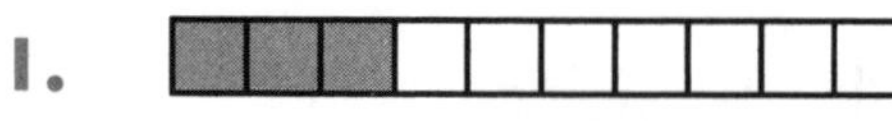		
	_____ or _____	_____ or _____	_____ or _____

Write the decimal equivalent to the given fraction.

	a	b	c	d
2.	$\frac{2}{10}$ = ___	$\frac{6}{10}$ = ___	$\frac{9}{10}$ = ___	$\frac{4}{10}$ = ___
3.	$\frac{3}{100}$ = ___	$\frac{4}{1,000}$ = ___	$\frac{8}{100}$ = ___	$\frac{5}{1,000}$ = ___

Locate $\frac{2}{10}$ and 0.8 on the number line.

4.

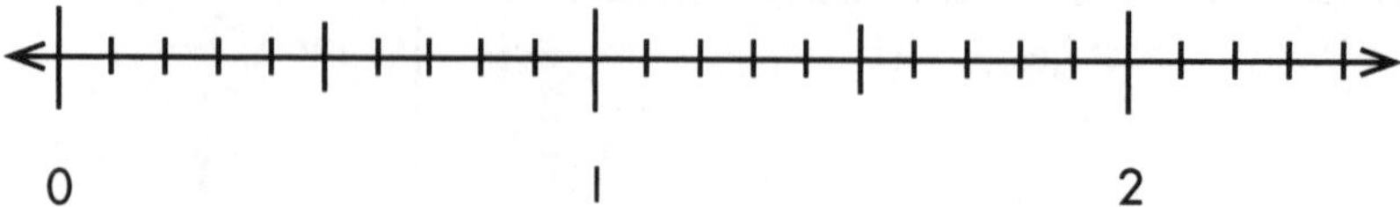

NAME ______________________________

Lesson 6.9 Understanding Decimals to Hundredths

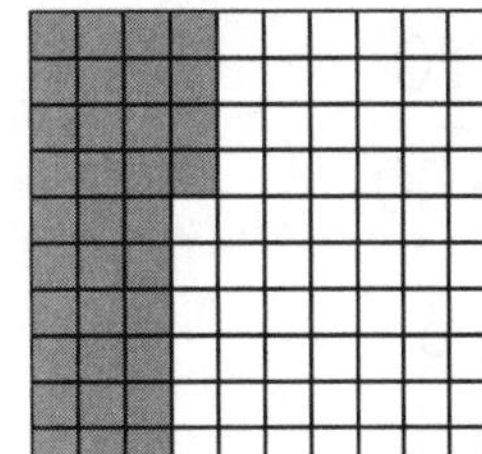

$\frac{34}{100}$ of the box is shaded. $\frac{34}{100}$ = four tenths = 0.34

$\frac{66}{100}$ of the box is unshaded. $\frac{6}{100}$ = six tenths = 0.66

Locate on a number line.

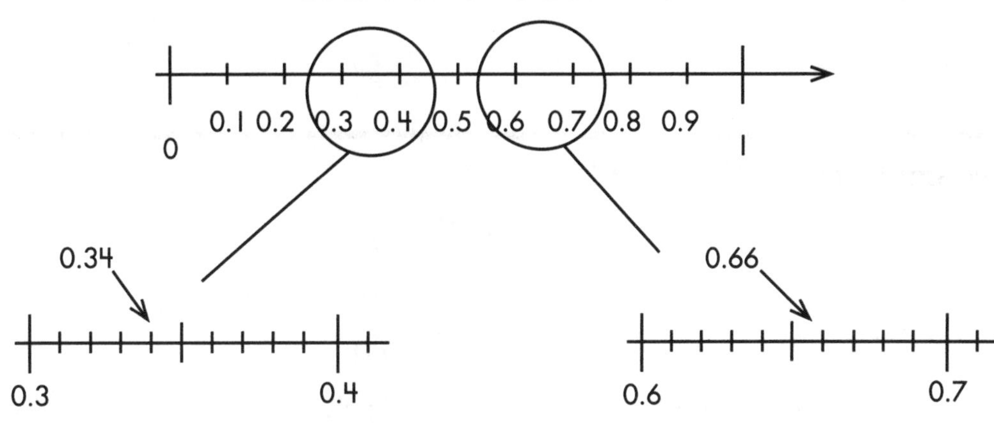

Write the decimal and fraction for each box.

1.

a

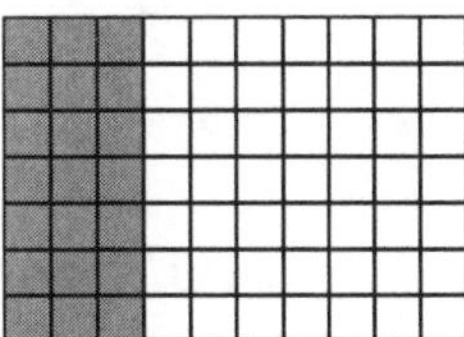

_____ or _____

b

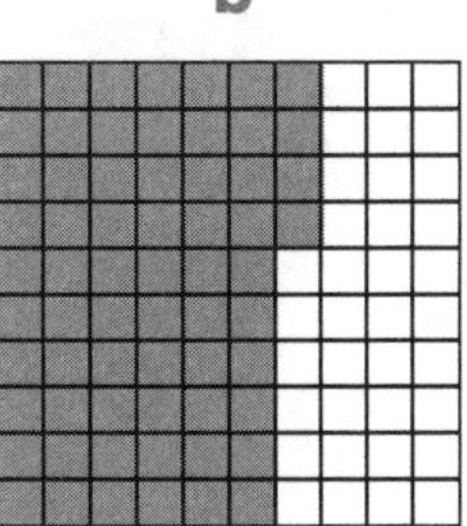

_____ or _____

c

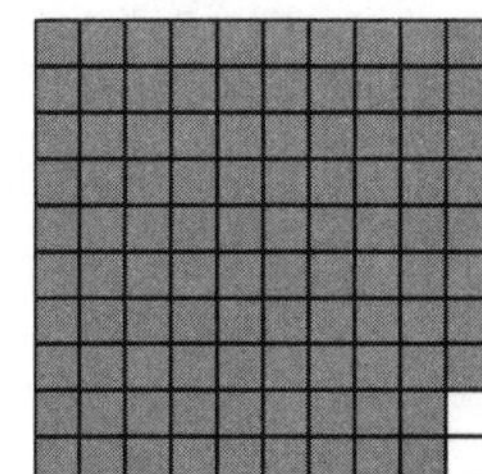

_____ or _____

Locate $\frac{47}{100}$ and 0.83 on the number line.

2.

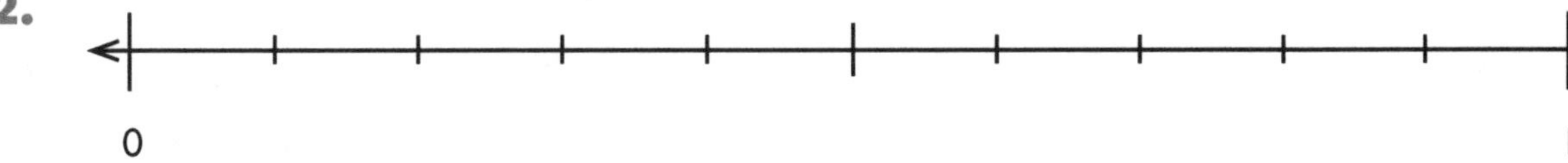

NAME ____________________

Lesson 6.10 Equivalent Fractions

$$\frac{1}{10} = \frac{10}{100}$$

because

$$\frac{1 \times 10}{10 \times 10} = \frac{10}{100}$$

Therefore...

$$\frac{1}{10} = \frac{10}{100}$$

$$+\ \frac{6}{100} = \frac{6}{100}$$

$$\frac{16}{100}$$

Find the equivalent fraction. Then, add.

	a	b	c	d
1.	$\frac{1}{10} + \frac{9}{100}$	$\frac{2}{10} + \frac{2}{100}$	$\frac{4}{10} + \frac{5}{100}$	$\frac{7}{10} + \frac{7}{100}$
2.	$\frac{5}{10} + \frac{50}{100}$	$\frac{1}{10} + \frac{1}{100}$	$\frac{4}{10} + \frac{8}{100}$	$\frac{6}{10} + \frac{5}{100}$
3.	$\frac{5}{10} + \frac{2}{100}$	$\frac{3}{10} + \frac{6}{100}$	$\frac{8}{10} + \frac{3}{100}$	$\frac{3}{10} + \frac{3}{100}$

NAME ______________________

Lesson 6.11 Adding Mixed Numerals with Like Denominators

$$\begin{array}{r} 3\frac{4}{9} \\ +\ 2\frac{2}{9} \\ \hline 5\frac{6}{9} = 5\frac{2}{3} \end{array}$$

Add the fractions. $\frac{4}{9} + \frac{2}{9} = \frac{6}{9}$

Add the whole numbers. $3 + 2 = 5$

Reduce to simplest form. $\frac{6 \div 3}{9 \div 3} = \frac{2}{3}$

Add. Write answers in simplest form.

	a	b	c	d	e
1.	$3\frac{4}{7} + 5\frac{3}{7}$	$6\frac{4}{9} + 8\frac{5}{9}$	$7\frac{1}{6} + 3\frac{1}{6}$	$2\frac{2}{5} + 4\frac{4}{5}$	$3\frac{2}{11} + 8\frac{8}{11}$
2.	$9\frac{3}{10} + 2\frac{9}{10}$	$5\frac{1}{8} + 4\frac{3}{8}$	$1\frac{6}{7} + 3\frac{2}{7}$	$8\frac{3}{4} + 6\frac{3}{4}$	$2\frac{2}{9} + 7\frac{2}{9}$
3.	$6\frac{4}{11} + 1\frac{3}{11}$	$3\frac{1}{10} + 4\frac{9}{10}$	$6\frac{5}{6} + 5\frac{5}{6}$	$5\frac{3}{8} + 8\frac{3}{8}$	$1\frac{5}{7} + 6\frac{4}{7}$
4.	$2\frac{11}{12} + 7\frac{11}{12}$	$8\frac{3}{5} + 8\frac{1}{5}$	$9\frac{5}{12} + 4\frac{7}{12}$	$2\frac{8}{9} + 5\frac{7}{9}$	$7\frac{9}{10} + 6\frac{9}{10}$

NAME ______________________

Lesson 6.12 Subtracting Mixed Numerals with Like Denominators

$$\begin{array}{rcr} 3\frac{2}{8} & = & 2\frac{10}{8} \\ -\,1\frac{3}{8} & = & -\,1\frac{3}{8} \\ \hline & & 1\frac{7}{8} \end{array}$$

$\frac{2}{8}$ is less than $\frac{3}{8}$. Rename $3\frac{3}{8}$.

Subtract the fractions.

Subtract the whole numbers.

$3 = 2 + 1 + \frac{2}{8}$

$= 2 + \frac{8}{8} + \frac{2}{8} = 2\frac{10}{8}$

Subtract. Write answers in simplest form.

	a	b	c	d	e
1.	$3\frac{3}{4} - 1\frac{1}{4}$	$6\frac{2}{7} - 2\frac{1}{7}$	$9\frac{7}{8} - 3\frac{5}{8}$	$8\frac{5}{6} - 4\frac{1}{6}$	$6\frac{5}{8} - 3\frac{3}{8}$
2.	$7\frac{7}{9} - 4\frac{4}{9}$	$5\frac{7}{10} - 3\frac{1}{10}$	$6\frac{3}{5} - 4\frac{2}{5}$	$9\frac{3}{7} - 7\frac{3}{7}$	$8\frac{7}{9} - 7\frac{2}{9}$
3.	$6\frac{4}{11} - 1\frac{3}{11}$	$4\frac{9}{10} - 3\frac{1}{10}$	$6\frac{5}{6} - 5\frac{5}{6}$	$8\frac{3}{8} - 5\frac{3}{8}$	$7\frac{5}{7} - 6\frac{4}{7}$
4.	$6\frac{3}{5} - 5\frac{1}{5}$	$4\frac{5}{7} - 1\frac{2}{7}$	$7\frac{9}{10} - 2\frac{3}{10}$	$8\frac{11}{12} - 1\frac{7}{12}$	$6\frac{8}{9} - 3\frac{7}{9}$

NAME ___________________________

Lesson 6.13 Problem Solving

SHOW YOUR WORK

Solve each problem. Write answers in simplest form.

1. It takes Carlos $2\frac{1}{6}$ days to make a model airplane and $1\frac{5}{6}$ days to make a model car. How many days will it take Carlos to make both?

   It will take __________ days for Carlos to make both.

2. Mr. Chen is going to the post office with two packages. One package weighs $6\frac{3}{8}$ kilograms and the other weighs $2\frac{1}{8}$ kilograms. How many kilograms are the two packages combined?

   The packages weigh __________ kilograms combined.

3. The beach is $6\frac{9}{10}$ miles from the Cabrera family. They have driven $2\frac{3}{10}$ miles toward the beach. How many more miles must the Cabrera family drive?

   The Cabrera family must drive __________ more miles.

4. Jaleela wants to paint her bedroom blue and gold. She has $4\frac{1}{8}$ gallons of blue paint and $2\frac{3}{8}$ gallons of gold paint. How much more blue paint does Jaleela have than gold paint?

   Jaleela has __________ more gallons of blue paint than gold paint.

5. Travis is $5\frac{7}{12}$ feet tall Nathan is $5\frac{11}{12}$ feet tall. How much taller is Nathan than Travis?

   Nathan is __________ foot taller than Travis.

1.
2.
3.
4.
5.

NAME ______________________________

Lesson 6.14 Fractions as Multiples

$\frac{4}{5} = 4 \times (\frac{1}{5})$ $\frac{1}{5} + \frac{1}{5} + \frac{1}{5} + \frac{1}{5} = \frac{4}{5}$

Write the addition equation and multiplication equation for each fraction.

1. $\frac{6}{10} = \_\_ \times (—)$ **OR**	**2.** $\frac{2}{8} = \_\_ \times (—)$ **OR**
3. $\frac{2}{4} = \_\_ \times (—)$ **OR**	**4.** $\frac{7}{3} = \_\_ \times (—)$ **OR**
5. $\frac{10}{6} = \_\_ \times (—)$ **OR**	**6.** $\frac{5}{12} = \_\_ \times (—)$ **OR**

NAME ______________________

Lesson 6.15 Multiplying Fractions and Whole Numbers

$\frac{2}{3} \times 6 = \frac{2}{3} \times \frac{6}{1}$	Rewrite the whole number as a fraction.	$7 \times \frac{1}{2} = \frac{7}{1} \times \frac{1}{2}$
$= \frac{2 \times 6}{3 \times 1}$	Multiply the numerators. Multiply the denominators.	$= \frac{7 \times 1}{1 \times 2}$
$= \frac{12}{3}$		$= \frac{7}{2}$
$= 4$	Reduce to simplest form.	$= 3\frac{1}{2}$

Multiply. Write answers in simplest form.

	a	b	c	d
1.	$3 \times \frac{1}{8} =$ ____	$5 \times \frac{2}{3} =$ ____	$\frac{2}{9} \times 8 =$ ____	$\frac{4}{7} \times 2 =$ ____
2.	$6 \times \frac{3}{5} =$ ____	$2 \times \frac{5}{9} =$ ____	$\frac{2}{7} \times 3 =$ ____	$7 \times \frac{3}{4} =$ ____
3.	$\frac{8}{9} \times 4 =$ ____	$\frac{1}{2} \times 8 =$ ____	$\frac{4}{5} \times 6 =$ ____	$9 \times \frac{1}{3} =$ ____
4.	$5 \times \frac{3}{10} =$ ____	$\frac{2}{3} \times 3 =$ ____	$9 \times \frac{7}{8} =$ ____	$\frac{6}{11} \times 7 =$ ____
5.	$\frac{4}{9} \times 7 =$ ____	$9 \times \frac{3}{10} =$ ____	$2 \times \frac{7}{12} =$ ____	$\frac{5}{7} \times 8 =$ ____

NAME ____________________

Lesson 6.15 Multiplying Fractions and Whole Numbers

Multiply. Write answers in simplest form.

	a	b	c	d
1.	$5 \times \frac{2}{7} =$ ____	$3 \times \frac{4}{5} =$ ____	$7 \times \frac{6}{8} =$ ____	$2 \times \frac{3}{4} =$ ____
2.	$4 \times \frac{2}{7} =$ ____	$6 \times \frac{1}{8} =$ ____	$8 \times \frac{1}{3} =$ ____	$2 \times \frac{3}{10} =$ ____
3.	$\frac{8}{9} \times 3 =$ ____	$\frac{2}{5} \times 5 =$ ____	$4 \times \frac{3}{8} =$ ____	$6 \times \frac{1}{8} =$ ____
4.	$3 \times \frac{5}{8} =$ ____	$4 \times \frac{1}{6} =$ ____	$\frac{1}{3} \times 9 =$ ____	$\frac{5}{9} \times 7 =$ ____
5.	$\frac{7}{12} \times 2 =$ ____	$3 \times \frac{6}{7} =$ ____	$\frac{1}{2} \times 5 =$ ____	$6 \times \frac{2}{3} =$ ____
6.	$\frac{1}{5} \times 4 =$ ____	$5 \times \frac{2}{3} =$ ____	$\frac{2}{7} \times 6 =$ ____	$3 \times \frac{2}{5} =$ ____

NAME ___________________________

Lesson 6.16 Problem Solving

SHOW YOUR WORK

Multiply. Write answers in simplest form.

1. One serving of pancakes calls for $\frac{1}{3}$ cup of milk. How many cups of milk are needed for 4 servings of pancakes?

_________ cups of milk are needed for four servings of pancakes.

2. If Carlos works $\frac{5}{12}$ of a day every day, how much will Carlos have worked after 5 days?

Carlos will have worked _________ days.

3. Tony had $1\frac{1}{2}$ gallons of orange juice. He drank $\frac{2}{7}$ of the orange juice he had. How much orange juice did Tony drink?

Tony drank _________ of a gallon of juice.

4. Miranda has 3 kites. Each kite needs $\frac{2}{3}$ yard of string. How much string does Miranda need for all 3 kites?

Miranda needs _________ yards of string.

5. A single serving of gelatin dessert requires $\frac{3}{8}$ cup sugar. How much sugar is needed for 6 servings?

_________ cups are needed.

6. Every day Sheila runs $\frac{4}{7}$ mile. If she runs for 9 days, how far will Sheila have run?

She will have run _________ miles.

7. Jason put down tile floor in his basement. He placed 18 tiles across the floor. Each tile is $12\frac{5}{8}$ inches wide. How wide is the area he covered with tiles?

The area covered with tiles is _________ inches in width.

1.

2.

3.

4.

5.

6.

7.

NAME ______________________

Check What You Learned

Fractions

Find the equivalent fraction.

1.

a	b	c	d
$\frac{3}{5} = \frac{\_\_}{25}$	$\frac{2}{6} = \frac{\_\_}{18}$	$\frac{1}{2} = \frac{9}{\_\_}$	$\frac{2}{8} = \frac{10}{\_\_}$

Compare the fractions using <, >, or =.

2.

a	b	c
$\frac{1}{5}$ ◯ $\frac{2}{10}$	$\frac{3}{4}$ ◯ $\frac{1}{2}$	$\frac{7}{10}$ ◯ $\frac{3}{5}$

Add or subtract.

3.

a	b	c	d
$\frac{1}{4} + \frac{1}{4}$	$\frac{8}{9} - \frac{1}{9}$	$\frac{5}{12} + \frac{3}{12}$	$\frac{5}{10} - \frac{3}{10}$

Decompose the fraction.

4. $\frac{3}{5}$

Write the decimal equivalent to the given fraction.

5. $\frac{8}{100}$ = ______

6. $\frac{4}{10}$ = ______

NAME ____________________

Check What You Learned

Fractions

Add or subtract.

	a	b	c	d
7.	$\frac{6}{10} + \frac{5}{100}$	$6\frac{2}{7} - 2\frac{1}{7}$	$6\frac{4}{11} + 1\frac{3}{11}$	$6\frac{8}{9} - 3\frac{7}{9}$
8.	$\frac{3}{10} + \frac{3}{100}$	$7\frac{7}{9} - 4\frac{4}{9}$	$6\frac{3}{5} - 5\frac{1}{5}$	$3\frac{4}{7} + 5\frac{3}{7}$

CHAPTER 6 POSTTEST

Multiply.

	a	b	c	d
9.	$8 \times \frac{8}{9} =$ ____	$\frac{5}{12} \times 6 =$ ____	$\frac{3}{8} \times 3 =$ ____	$7 \times \frac{4}{11} =$ ____
10.	$\frac{1}{4} \times 3 =$ ____	$\frac{1}{2} \times 9 =$ ____	$2 \times \frac{3}{5} =$ ____	$4 \times \frac{7}{10} =$ ____

NAME ______________________

Check What You Know

Measurement

Complete the following.

	a	b
1.	36 inches = ______ yard	8 quarts = ______ gallons
2.	1 cup = ______ ounces	1 mile = ______ yards
3.	2 feet = ______ inches	10 cups = ______ pints
4.	3 feet = ______ yard	8 pints = ______ quarts
5.	10 pints = ______ cups	8 cups = ______ quarts

Find the area and perimeter of each shape.

6.

30 yd.

10 yd. 10 yd.

30 yd.

A = ______ square yards
P = ______ yards

A = ______ square inches
P = ______ inches

Measure the angle.

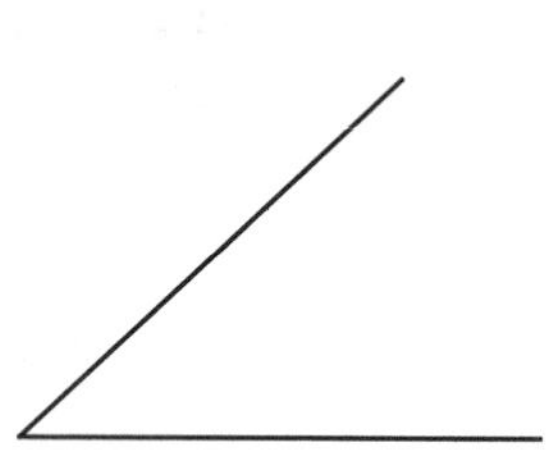

7. ________ °   **8.** ________ °   **9.** ________ °

NAME ____________________

Check What You Know

Measurement

SHOW YOUR WORK

CHAPTER 7 PRETEST

Solve each problem.

10. Paul is using a 4-quart container to fill a wash tub. If he needs 12 gallons of water to fill the tub, how many times does he need to fill the 4-quart container?

He needs to fill the container __________ times.

11. A worker at the zoo measured the length of an iguana. The iguana measured 72 inches long. How many feet did the iguana measure?

The iguana measured __________ feet.

12. The feed store has a half ton of wood shavings to ship to the horse farm. How many pounds of shavings does the feed store have?

The feed store has __________ pounds of wood shavings.

13. The town of Yarmouth is planning a skateboard park and needs to know the perimeter of the park. The property measures 7 yards by 3 yards by 10 yards by 5 yards. What is the perimeter?

The park's perimeter is __________ yards.

14. The Garcia brothers are painting a wall in their living room. The wall measures 8 feet by 10 feet. What is the area of the wall?

The area of the wall is __________ square feet.

10.
11.
12.
13.
14.

NAME ______________________

Check What You Know

Measurement

Complete the following.

	a	b
15.	5 km = ______ m	60,000 mL = ______ L
16.	6 m = ______ cm	32 kg = ______ g
17.	72 cm = ______ mm	19 L = ______ mL
18.	1 g = ______ mg	100 cm = ______ m
19.	25 kg = ______ g	65 cm = ______ mm
20.	17 L = ______ mL	5,200 cm = ______ m
21.	7,000 mg = ______ g	25 km = ______ m
22.	200 mm = ______ cm	9,000 mL = ______ L

Use the line plot to answer the questions.

Miles Run

8	$8\frac{1}{4}$	$8\frac{2}{4}$	$8\frac{3}{4}$	9	$9\frac{1}{4}$	$9\frac{2}{4}$	$9\frac{3}{4}$	10
	x		x x x					x

23. What is the difference between the longest distance run and the shortest distance run?

______

24. If you add all the distances together, what would be the total distance run?

______

Find the missing angle.

25.

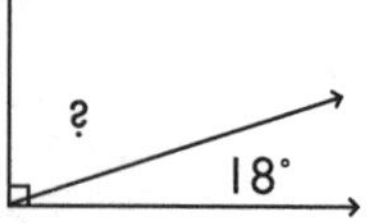

______

26.

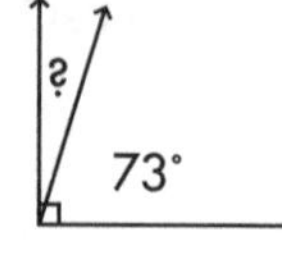

______

27.

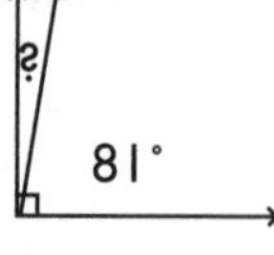

______

NAME ______________________

Check What You Know

Measurement

SHOW YOUR WORK

Solve each problem.

28. A hiking trail is 35 kilometers long. Sarah hiked 15 kilometers so far. How many more meters does Sarah have to hike?

Sarah has to hike __________ more meters.

29. The ham in the store weighs 1 kilogram, the turkey weighs 2 kilograms, and the chicken weighs 1 kilogram. How many grams do all three items in the grocery store weigh?

All three items weigh __________ kilograms.

30. Shawna needs liters of ginger ale and cola for a party, but it only comes in milliliters. If she orders 30,000 milliliters of ginger ale and 20,000 milliliters of cola, how many liters will she have?

She will have __________ liters.

31. The science experiment requires the students to measure 52,000 milligrams of chemicals. There are only 13,000 milligrams of chemicals in the science lab. How many more milligrams of chemicals do the students need?

The students need __________ more milligrams of chemicals.

28.

29.

30.

31.

NAME ___________________________

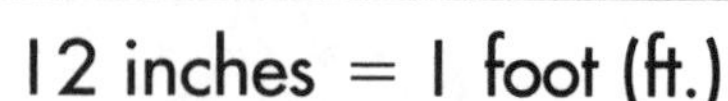

Units of Length (inches, feet, yards, and miles)

12 inches = 1 foot (ft.)
3 feet = 1 yard (yd.) 36 inches = 1 yard (yd.)
1,760 yards = 1 mile (mi.)
5,280 feet = 1 mile (mi.)

6 feet = ___ inches
(6 feet × 12 inches)
6 × 12 = 72
6 feet = 72 inches

72 feet = ___ yards

$$\begin{array}{r} 24 \\ 3\overline{)72} \\ \underline{6} \\ 12 \end{array}$$

72 feet = 24 yards

Complete the following.

	a	b	c
1.	5 yd. = ______ ft.	8 ft. = ______ in.	72 yd. = ______ ft.
2.	48 in. = ______ ft.	3 mi. = ______ yd.	24 yd. = ______ in.
3.	3,000 ft. = ______ yd.	24 in. = ______ ft.	2 mi. = ______ ft.
4.	12 in. = ______ ft.	26 yd. = ______ in.	12 ft. = ______ yd.
5.	360 in. = ______ yd.	10 ft. = ______ in.	720 yd. = ______ ft.
6.	7 mi. = ______ yd.	2,400 in. = ______ ft.	324 ft. = ______ yd.
7.	10 mi. = ______ ft.	600 in. = ______ ft.	6 ft. = ______ in.
8.	132 in. = ______ ft.	50 yd. = ______ in.	36 in. = ______ ft.
9.	72 ft. = ______ yd.	36 in. = ______ yd.	3,636 in. = ______ ft.
10.	8 mi. = ______ yd.	48 ft. = ______ yd.	120 in. = ______ ft.

NAME ______________________

Lesson 7.2 Problem Solving

SHOW YOUR WORK

Solve each problem.

1. Brandy has a curvy slide that is 5 feet long. Pedro has a curvy slide that is 8 feet long. How many inches longer is Pedro's slide than Brandy's slide?

Pedro's slide is __________ inches longer.

2. Kristi and Brian were competing in the long jump. Kristi jumped 9 feet. Brian jumped 6 feet. How many total yards did Kristi and Brian jump together?

They jumped a total of __________ yards.

3. The new speedboat measures 25 yards long. The old speedboat measured 18 yards long. How many feet longer is the new speedboat than the old speedboat?

The new speedboat is __________ feet longer.

4. The brown snake measures 12 feet long. The green snake measures 15 feet long. How many yards long are both the brown snake and the green snake?

Both snakes together are __________ yards long.

5. The hot air balloon traveled 15 miles on Monday and 18 miles on Tuesday. It still has 25 more miles to go to get to its destination. At the end of the trip, how many yards will the hot air balloon have traveled?

It will have traveled __________ yards.

6. David's flying disc soared for 468 feet. David picked it up and threw it again, and it soared for 375 feet. How many total yards did David's flying disc soar?

David's disc soared for __________ yards.

Show your work
1.
2.
3.
4.
5.
6.

NAME ______________________________

Lesson 7.3 Liquid Volume (cups, pints, quarts, and gallons)

Conversion Table

| cup (c.) = 8 ounces (oz.)
1 pint (pt.) = 2 cups (c.)
1 quart (qt.) = 2 pints (pt.)
1 quart (qt.) = 4 cups (c.)
1 gallon (gal.) = 4 quarts (qt.)
1 gallon (gal.) = 8 pints (pt.)
1 gallon (gal.) = 16 cups (c.)

When converting from more to less, multiply.

7 qt. = ______ pt.
Know: 1 qt. = 2 pt.
$7 \times 2 = 14$
7 qt. = 14 pt.

When converting from less to more, divide.

16 qt. = ______ gal.
Know: 4 qt. = 1 gal.
$16 \div 4 = 4$
16 qt. = 4 gal.

Complete the following.

	a	b	c
1.	2 gal. = ______ qt.	4 pt. = ______ qt.	12 c. = ______ pt.
2.	24 qt. = ______ gal.	16 oz. = ______ c.	10 qt. = ______ pt.
3.	14 pt. = ______ qt.	28 qt. = ______ gal.	14 pt. = ______ c.
4.	48 c. = ______ pt.	32 oz. = ______ c.	14 c. = ______ pt.
5.	10 gal. = ______ qt.	30 pt. = ______ c.	18 c. = ______ pt.
6.	12 gal. = ______ qt.	22 pt. = ______ qt.	64 oz. = ______ c.
7.	30 pt. = ______ qt.	20 c. = ______ oz.	40 qt. = ______ gal.
8.	18 c. = ______ pt.	44 pt. = ______ c.	80 qt. = ______ pt.
9.	150 qt. = ______ pt.	200 c. = ______ pt.	40 c. = ______ oz.
10.	88 oz. = ______ c.	16 qt. = ______ gal.	50 qt. = ______ pt.

NAME ______________________

Lesson 7.4 Weight (ounces, pounds, and tons)

Conversion Table

one-half pound (lb.) = 8 ounces (oz.)

1 pound (lb.) = 16 ounces (oz.)

one-half ton (T.) = 1,000 pounds (lb.)

1 ton (T.) = 2,000 pounds (lb.)

When converting from more to less, multiply.

5 lb. = _____ oz.

Know:

1 lb. = 16 oz.

5 × 16 = 80

5 lb. = 80 oz.

When converting from less to more, divide.

6,000 lb. = _____ T.

Know:

2,000 lb. = 1 T.

6,000 ÷ 2,000 = 3

6,000 lb. = 3 T.

Complete the following.

	a	b	c
1.	32 oz. = ______ lb.	6,000 lb. = ______ T.	4 T. = ______ lb.
2.	40 lb. = ______ oz.	64 oz. = ______ lb.	24,000 lb. = ______ T.
3.	1,000 lb. = ______ T.	8 oz. = ______ lb.	18,000 lb. = ______ T.
4.	8 lb. = ______ oz.	12 lb. = ______ oz.	10,000 lb. = ______ T.

	Tons	Pounds	Ounces
5.	5	______	160,000
6.	______	4,000	64,000
7.	3	6,000	______
8.	4	8,000	______
9.	______	2,000	32,000
10.	6	12,000	______
11.	10	______	320,000

NAME ____________________

Lesson 7.5 Problem Solving

SHOW YOUR WORK

Solve each problem.

1. The cooks made 120 quarts of lemonade for the first concert. They made 150 quarts of lemonade for the second concert and 130 quarts for the third concert. How many gallons of lemonade did the cooks make for all three concerts?

They made __________ gallons of lemonade in all.

1.

2. A large ship was being loaded with 20 tons of grain and 5 tons of flour. How many more pounds of grain were there on the ship?

There were __________ more pounds of grain.

2.

3. The largest wheel of cheese in City A weighs 985 pounds. The largest wheel of cheese in City B weighs 894 pounds. How many total ounces do both wheels of cheese weigh?

They weigh a total of __________ ounces.

3.

4. Tito stored 15 gallons of water in his basement. Jack stored 29 gallons of water in his basement. During the hurricane, they used 32 gallons of water. How many quarts of water did the boys have left after the hurricane?

Tito and Jack had __________ quarts of water left.

4.

5. The large airplane carried 5 tons of luggage this week. The medium airplane carried 3 tons of luggage this week. The small airplane carried 1,544 pounds of luggage this week. How many total pounds of luggage did all 3 planes carry this week?

All three planes carried a total of __________ pounds of luggage this week.

5.

NAME ______________________________

Lesson 7.6 Measuring in Millimeters

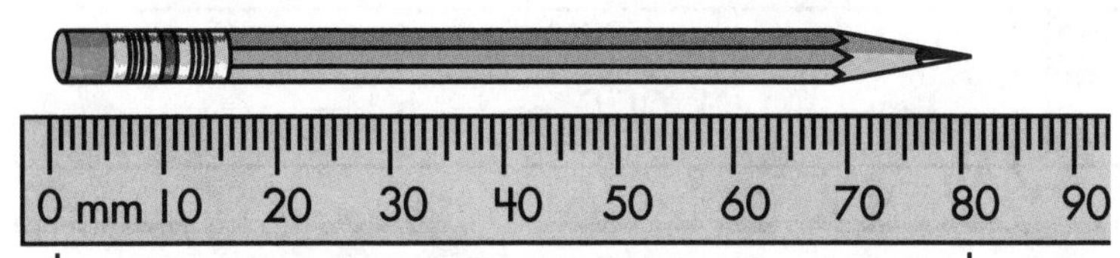

80 millimeters or 8 centimeters

The pencil is 8 centimeters or 80 millimeters long.

1 centimeter (cm) = 10 millimeters (mm)
1 cm = 10 mm

Use a ruler and pencil to finish the shape. Find the length of the missing side in millimeters.

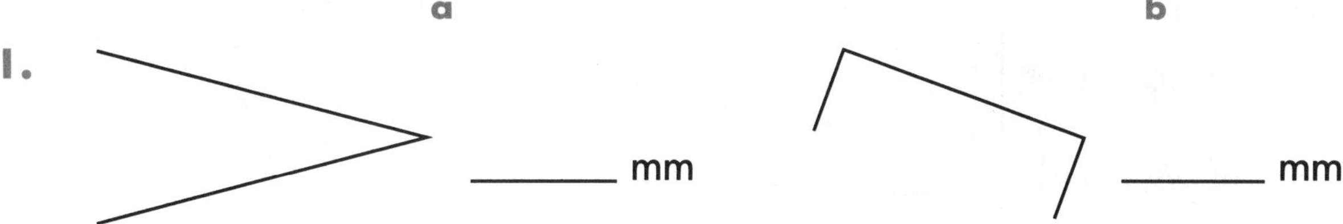

	a	b
1.	______ mm	______ mm
2.	______ mm	______ mm

Complete the following.

	a	b
3.	7 cm = ______ mm	2 cm = ______ mm
4.	5 cm = ______ mm	60 mm = ______ cm
5.	90 mm = ______ cm	11 cm = ______ mm
6.	100 mm = ______ cm	25 cm = ______ mm

NAME ______________________

Lesson 7.7 Meters and Kilometers

100 centimeters (cm) = 1 meter (m) 100 cm = 1 m	1,000 meters (m) = 1 kilometer (km) 1,000 m = 1 km

Find the length of each of the following objects around your home to the nearest meter.

	Object	Length (m)
1.	width of TV screen	______ m
2.	height of stove	______ m
3.	height of computer	______ m
4.	width of your bed	______ m
5.	height of TV	______ m
6.	your height	______ m
7.	width of a window	______ m

Complete the following.

	a	b
8.	600 cm = ______ m	9,000 m = ______ km
9.	7 m = ______ cm	10,000 m = ______ km
10.	7 km = ______ m	23 km = ______ m
11.	8 m = ______ cm	32 m = ______ cm
12.	2 km = ______ m	14 m = ______ cm

NAME ___________________________

Lesson 7.8 Units of Length (millimeters, centimeters, meters, and kilometers)

7 cm = ___ mm	3 m = ___ mm	32 m = ___ cm	15 km = ___ m
1 cm = 10 mm	1 m = 1,000 mm	1 m = 100 cm	1 km = 1,000 m
$1 \times 7 = 7$; $10 \times 7 = 70$	$1 \times 3 = 3$; $1000 \times 3 = 3000$	$1 \times 32 = 32$; $100 \times 32 = 3200$	$1 \times 15 = 15$; $1000 \times 15 = 15000$
7 cm = 70 mm	3 m = 3,000 mm	32 m = 3,200 cm	15 km = 15,000 m

Complete the following.

	a	b
1.	4 m = ______ cm	25 m = ______ mm
2.	21 km = ______ m	25 cm = ______ mm
3.	33 m = ______ cm	14 km = ______ m
4.	15 m = ______ cm	47 m = ______ mm
5.	5 km = ______ m	84 cm = ______ mm
6.	75 m = ______ cm	72 m = ______ cm
7.	10 km = ______ m	66 m = ______ mm
8.	21 cm = ______ mm	19 km = ______ m

NAME ______________________

Lesson 7.9 Measuring Perimeter

Perimeter is the distance around a shape.

To calculate perimeter, add together the lengths of all the sides.

Perimeter = 17 in. + 10 in. + 17 in. + 10 in.

Perimeter = 54 in.

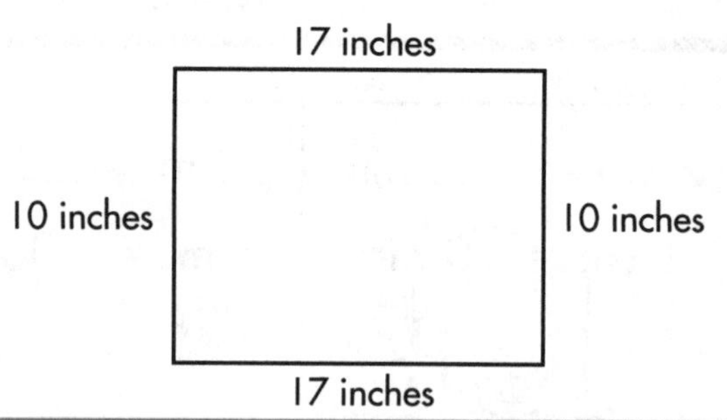

Find the perimeter of each shape.

1.

a

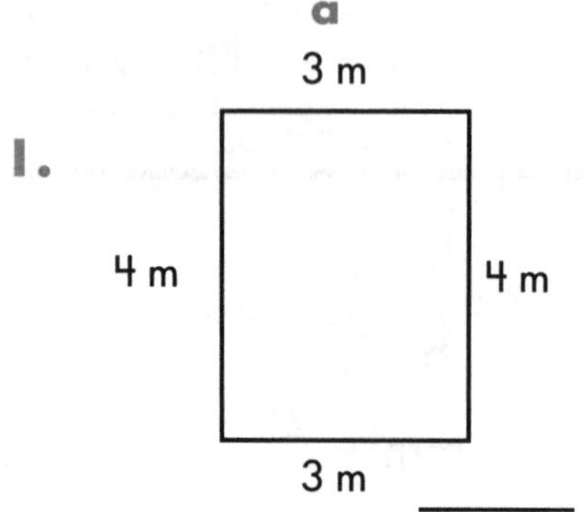

______ m

b

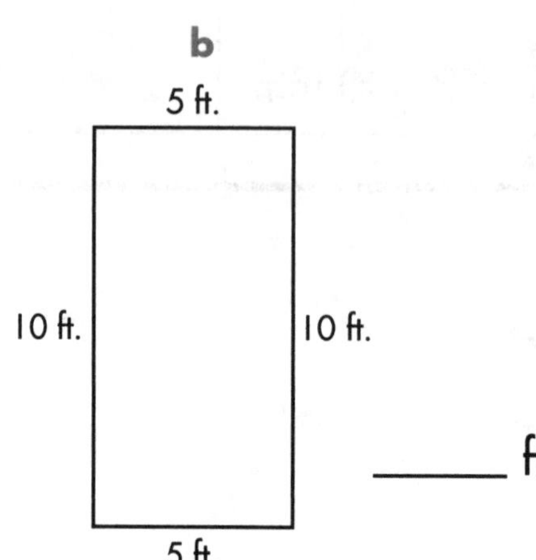

______ ft.

c

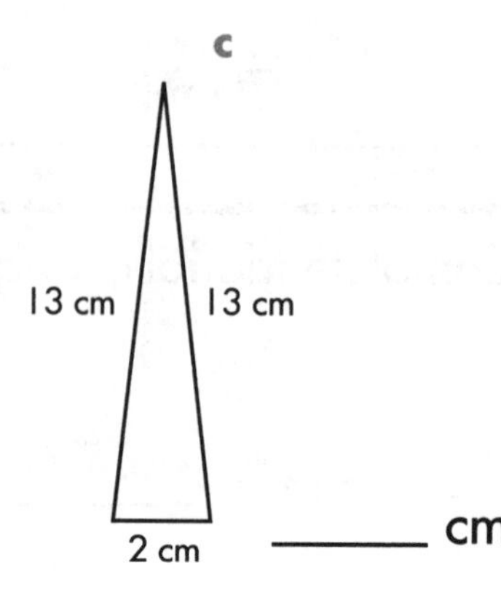

______ cm

2.

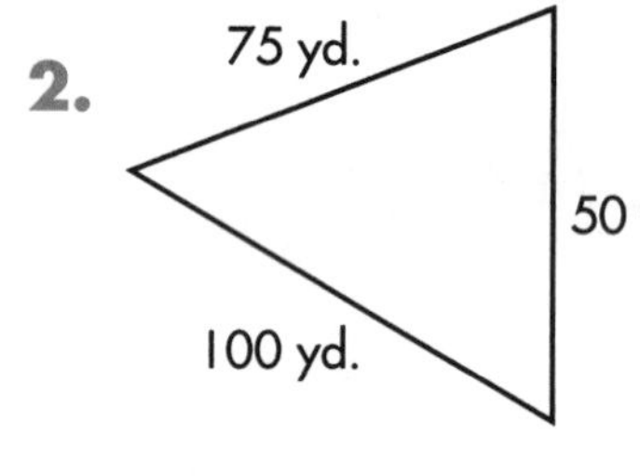

______ yd.

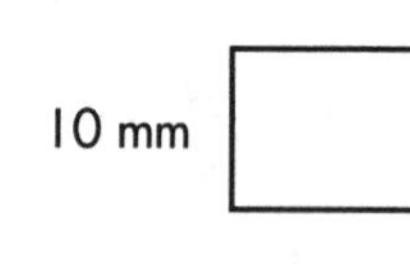

______ mm

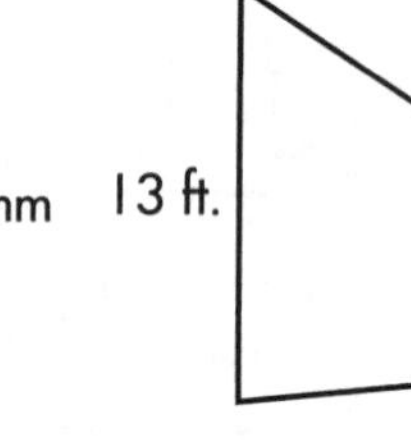
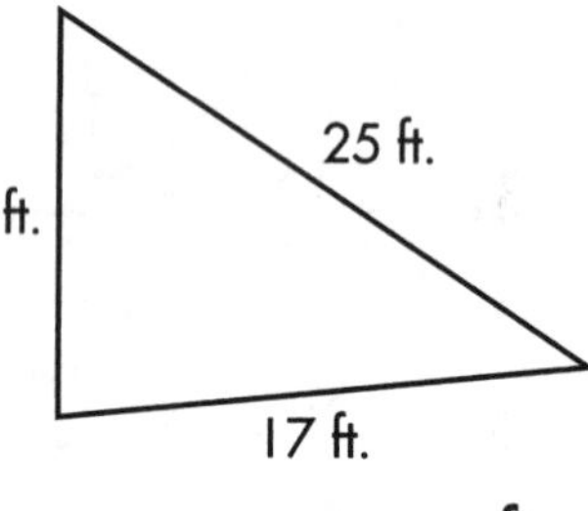

______ ft.

3.

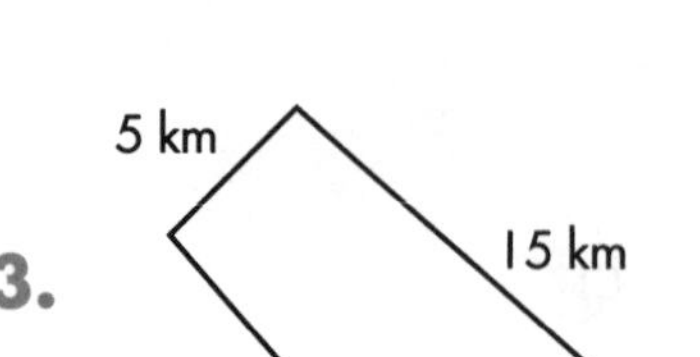

______ km

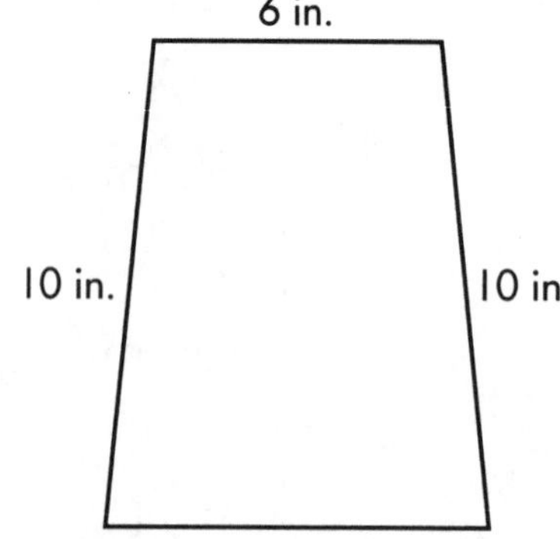

______ in.

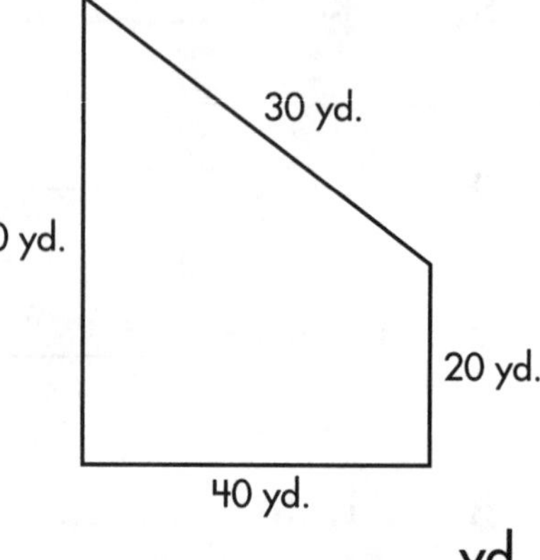

______ yd.

NAME ______________________________

Lesson 7.10 Measuring Area

Area is the amount of space a shape covers.
To find the area of a square or rectangle, multiply length by width.

Area = 100 ft. × 20 ft. = 2,000 sq. ft.

100 ft. (length)

20 ft. (width)

Find the area of each shape.

	a	b	c
1.	15 in. by 12 in.	12 mm by 12 mm 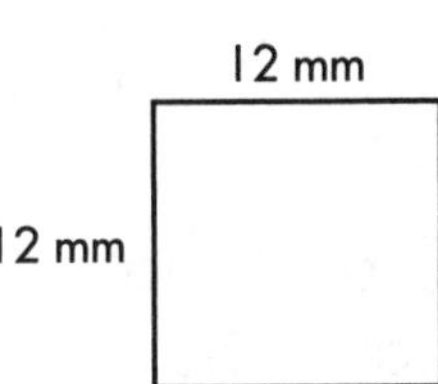	12 ft. by 11 ft. 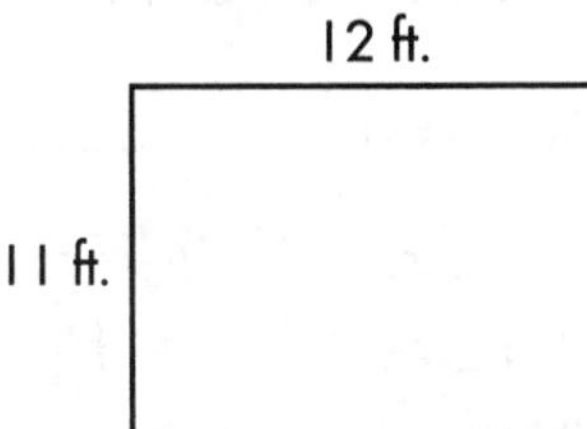
	______ sq. in.	______ sq. mm	______ sq. ft.
2.	10 yd. by 25 yd. 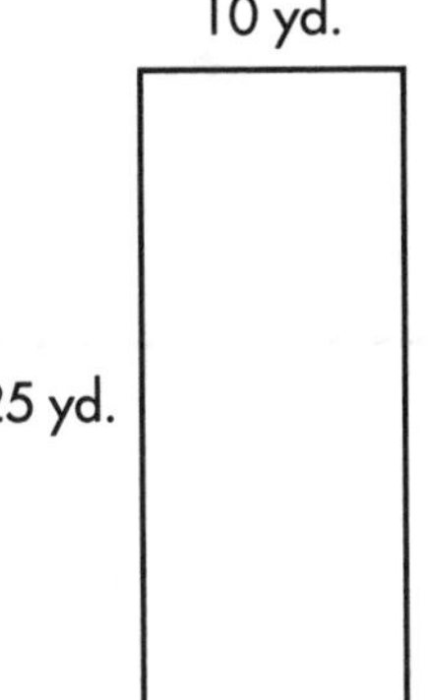	5 in. by 8 in. 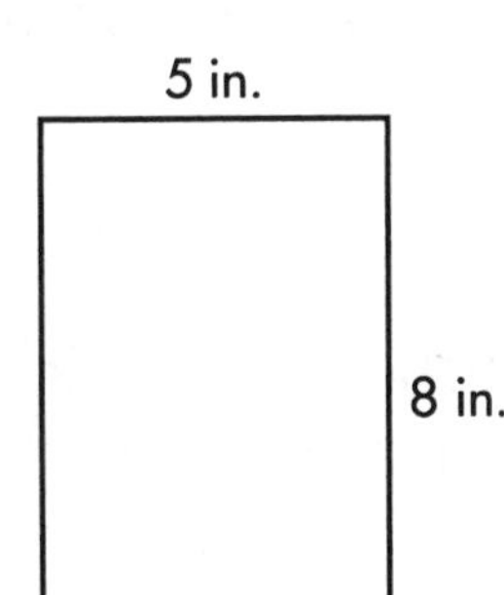	12 m by 40 m 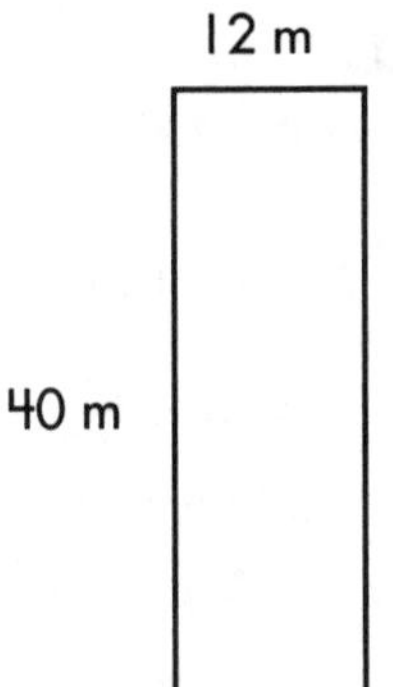
	______ sq. yd.	______ sq. in.	______ sq. m

	a	b
3.	23 yd. by 8 yd. 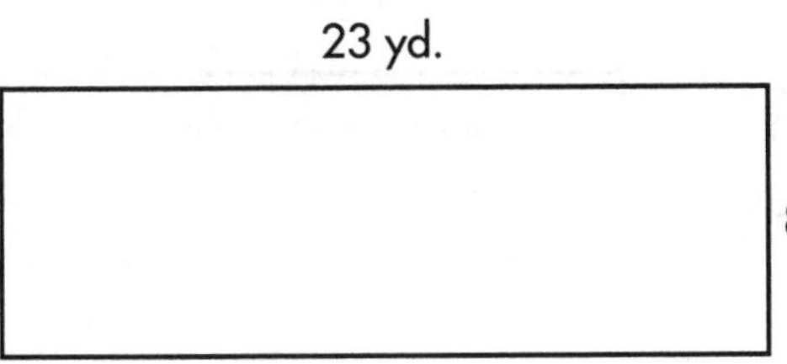	20 km by 4 km
	______ sq. yd.	______ sq. km

NAME ______________________

Lesson 7.11 Problem Solving

SHOW YOUR WORK

Solve each problem.

1. John cleared a vacant lot to plant a garden. The lot measured 35 feet by 15 feet. What is the perimeter of the garden lot?

   The perimeter of the lot is __________ feet.

2. Freda is putting carpet down in a room that measures 20 feet long by 30 feet wide. What is the area of the room?

   The area is __________ square feet.

3. The zoo is building a new hippo pool that will measure 55 feet by 75 feet. What is the area of the pool?

   The area is __________ square feet.

4. Gabriel built a cage for his tropical birds. The cage measures 14 feet by 12 feet. What is the perimeter of the cage?

   The perimeter of the cage is __________ feet.

5. The Foster's deck was almost finished. Each side of the square deck was 25 feet long. What was the area of the deck?

   The area was __________ square feet.

6. The length of the walking track is 103 feet and the width is 50 feet. What is the perimeter of the track?

   The perimeter is __________ feet.

7. The college donated land for a park. The land is 750 feet long and 25 feet wide. What is the area of the land?

   The area is __________ square feet.

1.
2.
3.
4.
5.
6.
7.

NAME ______________________

Lesson 7.12 Liquid Volume (milliliters)

1 liter (L) = 1,000 milliliters (mL)
1 L = 1,000 mL

4 liters = ___ milliliters

1 liter = 1,000 milliliters

$$\begin{array}{r} 1 \\ \times 4 \\ \hline 4 \end{array} \qquad \begin{array}{r} 1000 \\ \times \quad 4 \\ \hline 4000 \end{array}$$

4 liters = 4,000 milliliters

Complete the following.

	a	b	c
1.	3 L = ______ mL	12 L = ______ mL	2 L = ______ mL
2.	75 L = ______ mL	10 L = ______ mL	50 L = ______ mL
3.	13 L = ______ mL	78 L = ______ mL	8 L = ______ mL

SHOW YOUR WORK

Solve each problem.

4. A pool for the dogs needs 75 liters of water. How many milliliters of water are needed?

   ________ milliliters of water are needed.

5. Mitchell is making punch and needs 7,000 milliliters of pineapple juice. How many liters of juice does he need?

   He needs ________ liters of juice.

6. The pitcher holds 2 liters. How many pitchers does José need to fill a 24-liter punch bowl?

   José needs ________ pitchers to fill the bowl.

4.

5.

6.

NAME ____________________

Lesson 7.13 Weight (milligrams, grams, and kilograms)

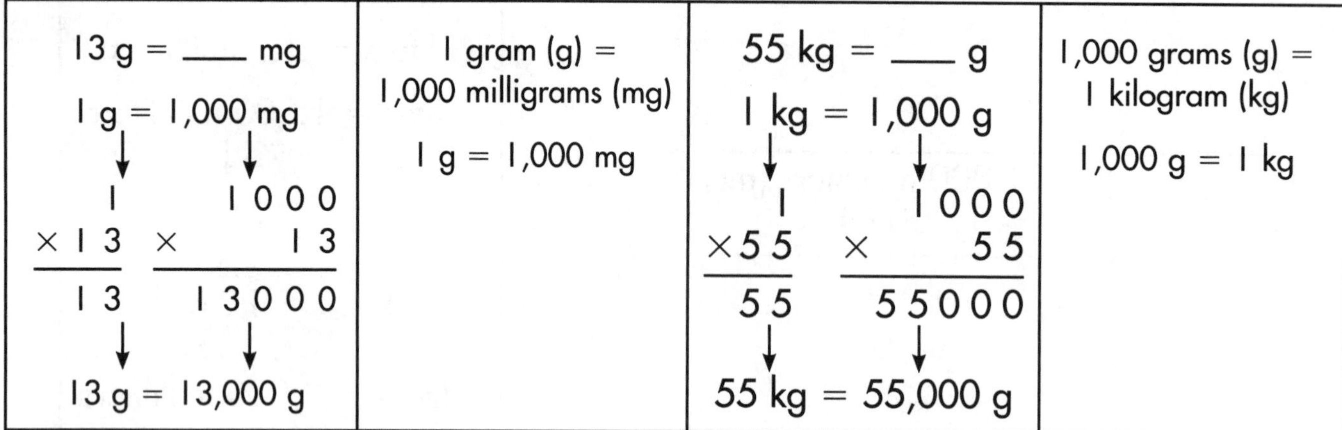

13 g = ___ mg 1 g = 1,000 mg 1 × 13 = 13 1000 × 13 = 13000 13 g = 13,000 g	1 gram (g) = 1,000 milligrams (mg) 1 g = 1,000 mg	55 kg = ___ g 1 kg = 1,000 g 1 × 55 = 55 1000 × 55 = 55000 55 kg = 55,000 g	1,000 grams (g) = 1 kilogram (kg) 1,000 g = 1 kg

Complete the following.

	a	b	c
1.	6 kg = ______ g	32 g = ______ mg	45 kg = ______ g
2.	10 g = ______ mg	42 kg = ______ g	9 g = ______ mg
3.	105 g = ______ mg	37 g = ______ mg	12 kg = ______ g
4.	183 kg = ______ g	18 g = ______ mg	119 kg = ______ g

SHOW YOUR WORK

Solve each problem.

5. The bags Jon carries weigh 45,000 mg each. How many grams does each bag weigh?

Each bag weighs ________ grams.

6. Teresa's vitamins contain 7,000 milligrams of vitamin E. How many grams of vitamin E does Teresa take in each vitamin?

Teresa takes ________ grams.

5.

6.

NAME ______________________

Lesson 7.14 Line Plots in Measurement

Use the table to complete the line plot. Then, answer the questions.

Lengths of Books on a Shelf in Inches	
5	||||
$5\frac{1}{2}$	|||
6	||
$6\frac{1}{2}$	~~||||~~
7	~~||||~~

Lengths of Books on a Shelf in Inches

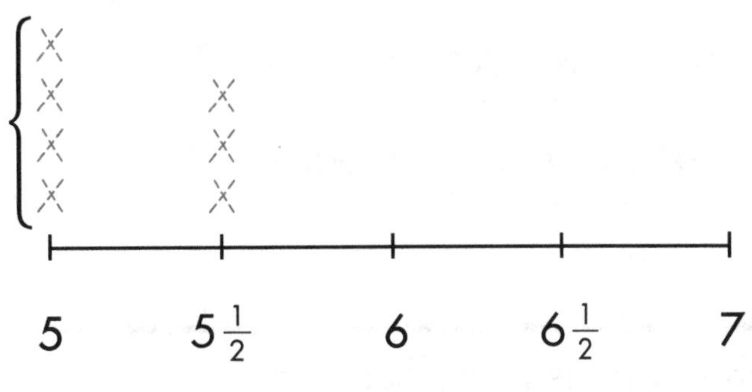

5 $5\frac{1}{2}$ 6 $6\frac{1}{2}$ 7

1. What is the difference between the longest and shortest books?

____

2. How many books measured 6 inches?

____

Cups of Sugar Used in Cookies	
$4\frac{1}{2}$	||
5	
$5\frac{1}{2}$	
6	
$6\frac{1}{2}$	||
7	

Cups of Sugar Used in Cookies

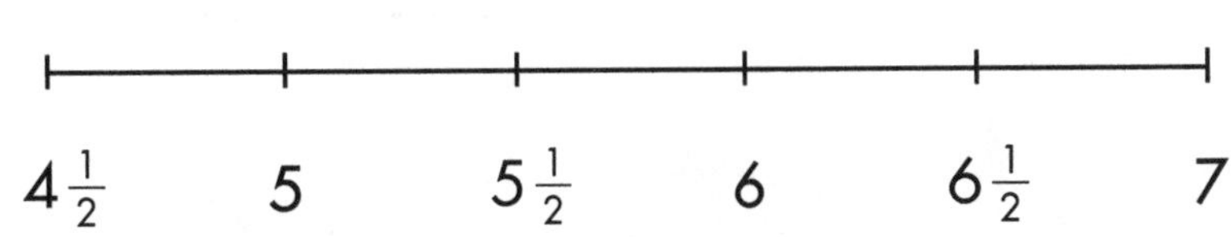

$4\frac{1}{2}$ 5 $5\frac{1}{2}$ 6 $6\frac{1}{2}$ 7

3. How many total cups of sugar were used to make cookies?

____

NAME ____________________

Lesson 7.15 Measuring Angles

A **protractor** is used to measure an angle. The angle is measured in degrees.

A **right angle** measures exactly 90°.

An **acute angle** measures less than 90°.

An **obtuse angle** measures greater than 90° but less than 180°.

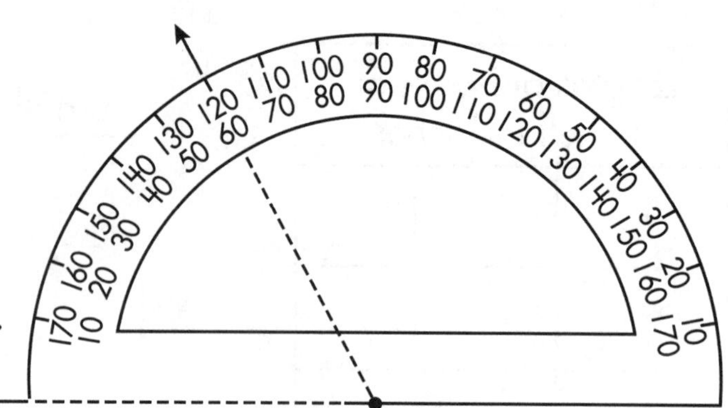

Identify each angle as *right*, *acute*, or *obtuse*.

	a	Type of Angle	b	Type of Angle
1.	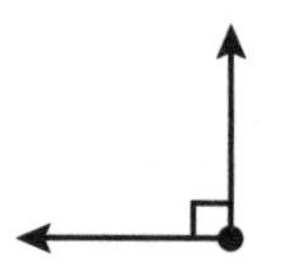	________		________
2.	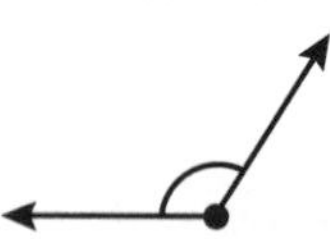	________	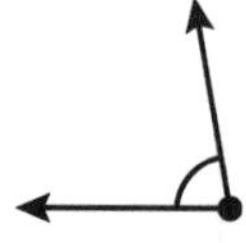	________
3.	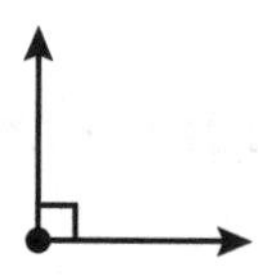	________		________

Lesson 7.16 Measuring and Drawing Angles

Use a protractor to measure each angle.

	a	b
1.	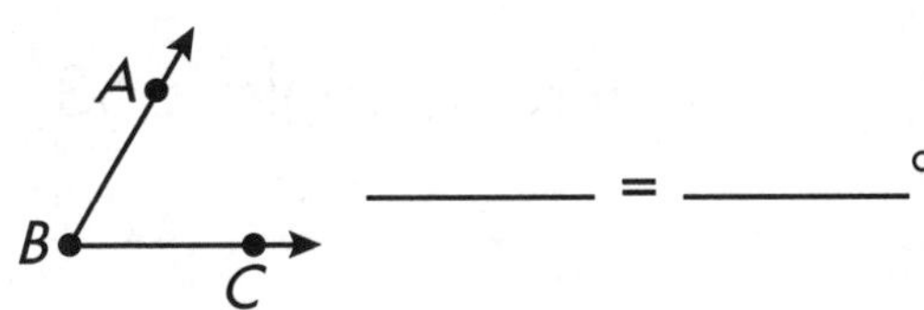 ______ = ______°	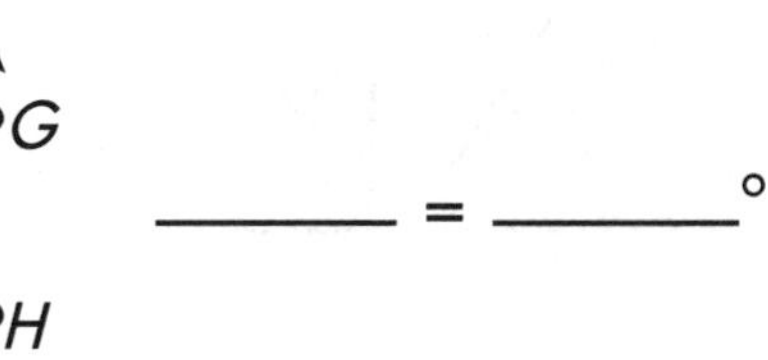 ______ = ______°
2.	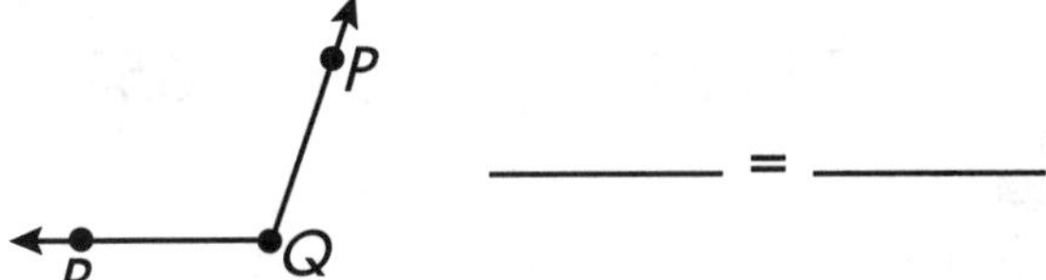 ______ = ______°	X Y Z ______ = ______°
3.	 ______ = ______°	A C B ______ = ______°

Draw an angle that measures the degrees given.

4. 90°	**5.** 50°	**6.** 125°

NAME ____________________

Lesson 7.17 Finding Missing Angles

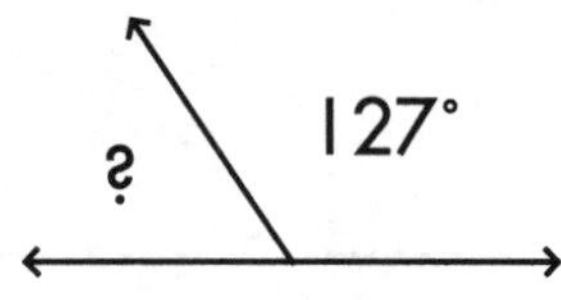

To find the missing angle in a straight angle, subtract the given angle from 180°.

$$\begin{array}{r} \overset{7\,10}{1\cancel{8}\cancel{0}}^\circ \\ -\ 127^\circ \\ \hline 53^\circ \end{array}$$

The missing angle is 53°.

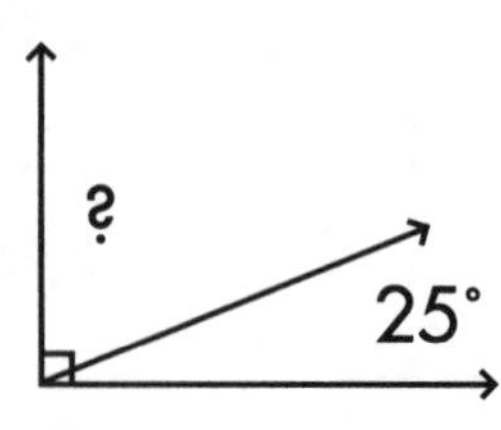

To find the missing angle in a right angle, subtract the given angle from 90°.

$$\begin{array}{r} \overset{8\,10}{\cancel{9}\cancel{0}}^\circ \\ -\ 25^\circ \\ \hline 65^\circ \end{array}$$

The missing angle is 65°.

Find the value of the missing angles.

	a		b	
1.	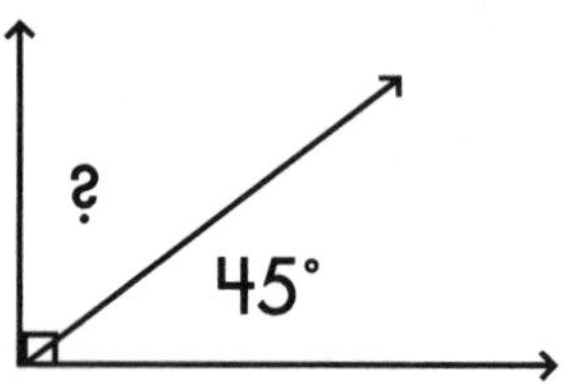 ? 45°	________	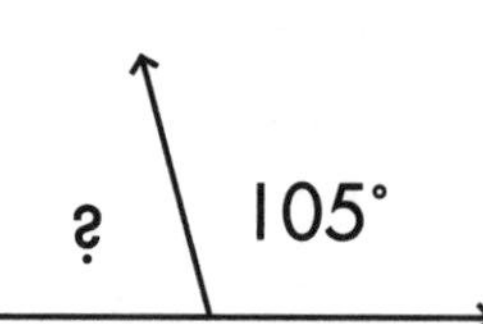 ? 105°	________
2.	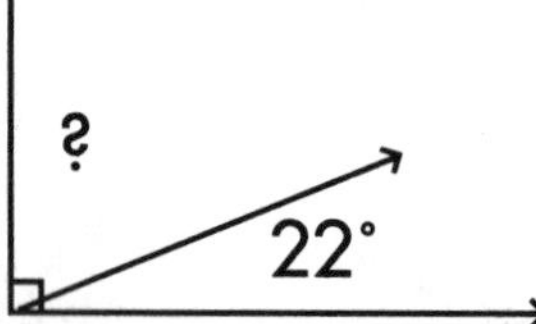 ? 22°	________	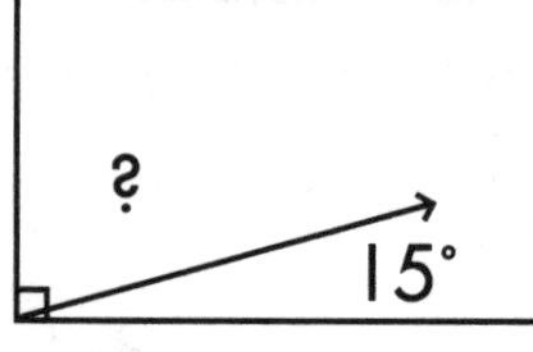 ? 15°	________
3.	 ? 92°	________	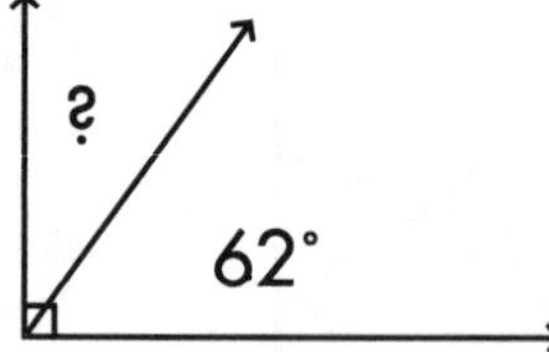 ? 62°	________
4.	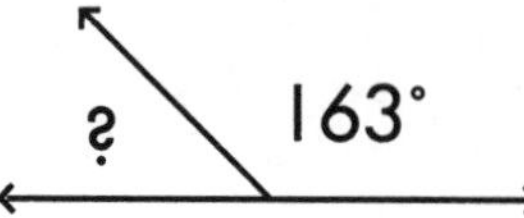 ? 163°	________	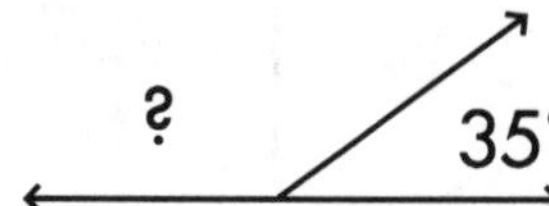 ? 35°	________

NAME ______________________

Check What You Learned

Measurement

Complete the following.

	a	b	c
1.	4 ft. = ______ in.	5 lb. = ______ oz.	2 T. = ______ lb.
2.	4 qt. = ______ gal.	72 oz. = ______ c.	15 yd. = ______ ft.
3.	5,280 yd. = ______ mi.	17 pt. = ______ c.	80 oz. = ______ lb.

Find the perimeter of each shape.

4.

a

13 ft.

9 ft. 9 ft.

13 ft.

______ ft.

b

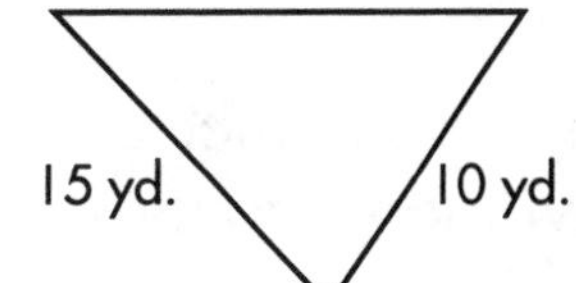

______ yd.

Find the area of each shape.

5.

13 ft.

30 ft.

______ sq. ft.

15 in.

15 in.

______ sq. in.

Find the measure of each angle.

6.

a

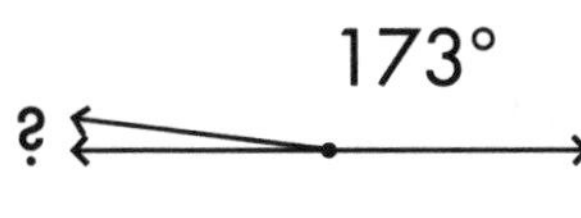

______

b

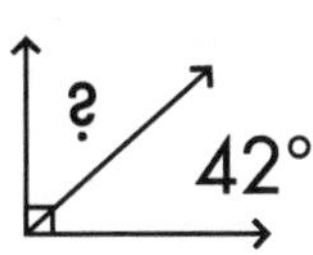

______

c

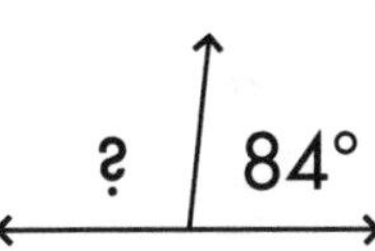

______

NAME ____________________

Check What You Learned

SHOW YOUR WORK

Measurement

Solve each problem.

7. The new refrigerator holds 16 quarts of juice. The old refrigerator held 2 quarts of juice. How many more gallons does the new refrigerator hold than the old one?

It holds __________ more gallons of juice.

8. The local dairy sold 60 pints of chocolate milk to one fourth grade class and 40 pints of milk to another fourth grade class. How many cups of milk did the dairy sell to both classes altogether?

The dairy sold __________ cups of milk in all.

9. At the store, a container of ice cream weighs 32 ounces. How many pounds do 4 containers of ice cream weigh?

Four containers weigh __________ pounds.

10. The area of a window measures 336 square inches. If the window is 16 inches wide, how long is the window?

The window is __________ inches long.

11. A swimming pool has a perimeter of 72 feet. The short sides measure 16 feet each. What is the length of the longer sides of the pool?

The longer sides of the pool measure __________ feet each.

7.
8.
9.
10.
11.

CHAPTER 7 POSTTEST

NAME ___________________________

Check What You Learned

Measurement

Complete the following.

	a	b
12.	600 mm = ______ cm	2,050 cm = ______ mm
13.	13 cm = ______ mm	4 m = ______ cm
14.	37 km = ______ m	15 L = ______ mL
15.	44 g = ______ mg	9 kg = ______ g
16.	95 m = ______ cm	220 cm = ______ mm
17.	5,000 m = ______ km	76 m = ______ cm
18.	56 m = ______ cm	232 km = ______ m
19.	865 cm = ______ mm	45 L = ______ mL
20.	267 g = ______ mg	26 kg = ______ g
21.	2 L = ______ mL	15 cm = ______ mm
22.	22 m = ______ mm	67 km = ______ m
23.	300 cm = ______ m	3,000 m = ______ km

Use the line plot to answer the questions.

Length of Sticks in Inches

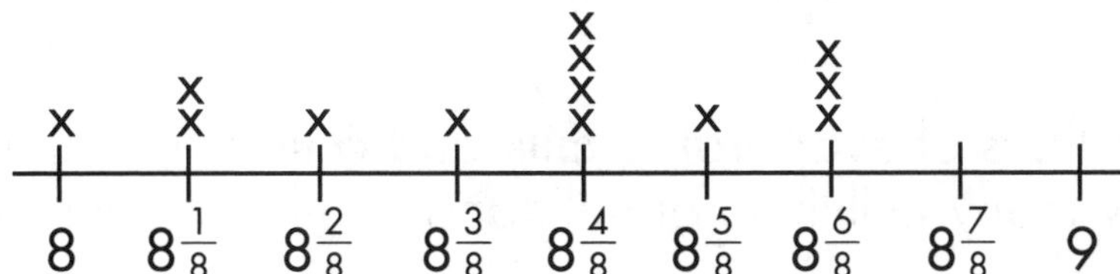

24. How many sticks measure $8\frac{4}{8}$ inches?

____

25. What is the difference between the longest stick measured and the shortest stick measured?

____

NAME ______________________

Check What You Learned

Measurement

Draw an angle that measures the degrees given.

	a	b	c
26.	90°	130°	175°

Find the missing angles

a **b**

27.

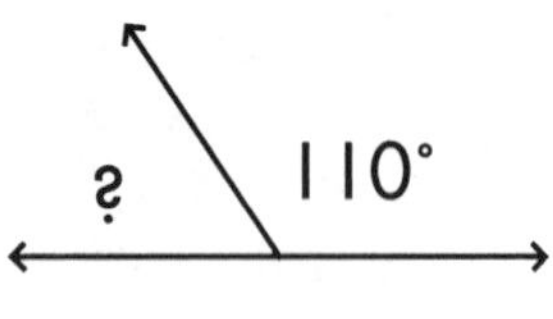

______

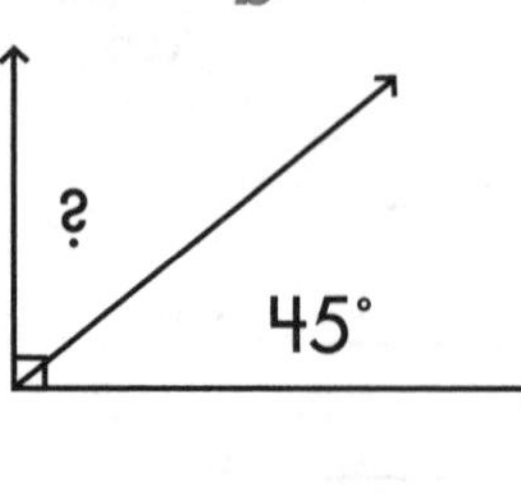

______

28.

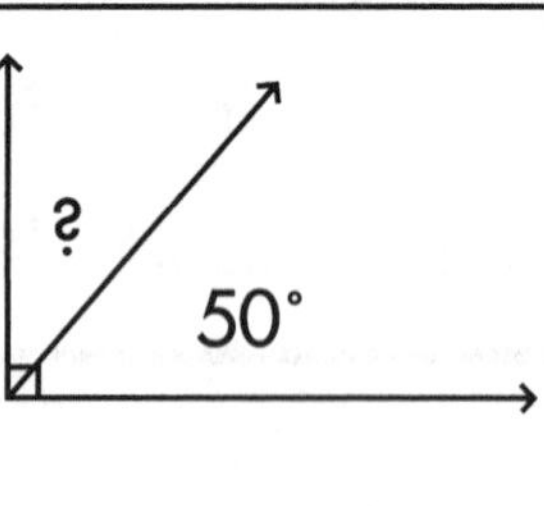

______

? 160°

______

Solve each problem.

29. A recipe listed 8 liters of evaporated milk and 6 liters of vanilla extract as ingredients. How many milliliters of milk and vanilla extract did the recipe call for?

The recipe called for ______ milliliters of milk and vanilla extract.

30. Bob ran 75 kilometers today and 62 kilometers the day before. How many meters did he run in all?

Bob ran ______ meters.

NAME ______________________

Check What You Know

Geometry

Identify the angles given.

1.

a

angle ______

b

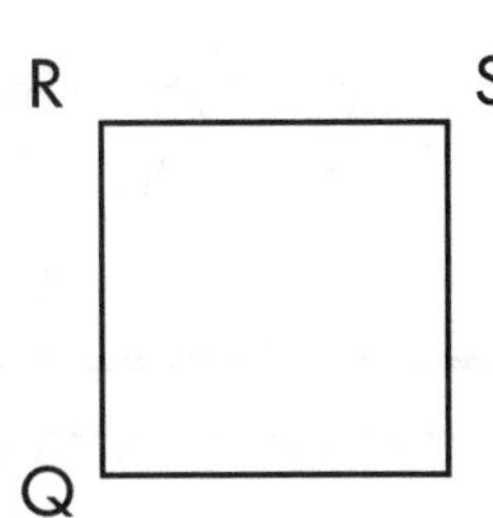

angle ______

Draw each type of line.

2.

a	b	c
parallel	perpendicular	intersecting

Draw the line (or lines) of symmetry for each figure.

3.

a

b

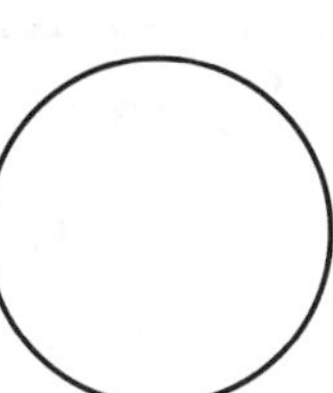

c

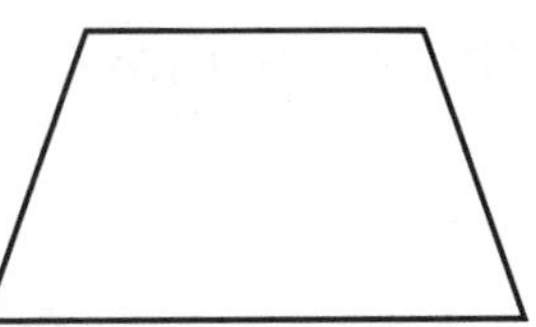

d

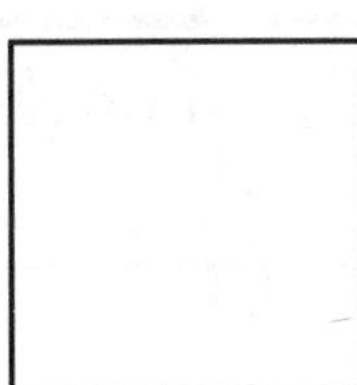

Identify the quadrilateral.

4.

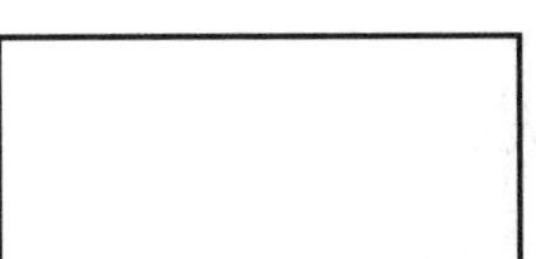

______

Identify the triangle.

5.

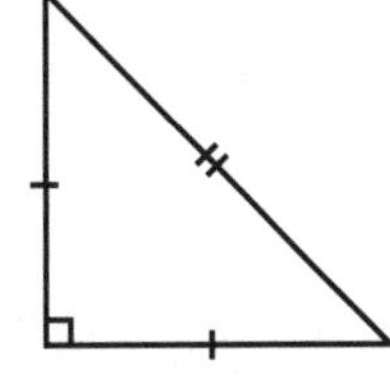

______

NAME ______________________

Lesson 8.1 Points, Lines, Rays, and Angles

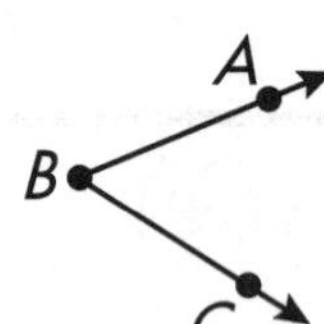

The **angle** ABC (denoted ∠ABC) is made of ray BA ($\overrightarrow{BA}$) and ray BC ($\overrightarrow{BC}$). The point where the two rays intersect is called the vertex. The **vertex** of ∠ABC is point B.

An angle can be measured using a **protractor**. A protractor measures angles that range from 0° to 180°.

Identify or draw the rays and vertex of each angle. Name or label the angle.

a | **b**

1.

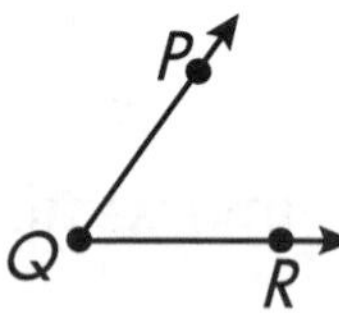

rays: ______
______
vertex: ______
angle: ______

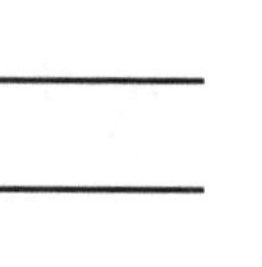

rays: ______
______
vertex: ______
angle: ______

2.

rays: $\overrightarrow{LM}$
$\overrightarrow{MN}$
vertex: M
angle: ∠LMN

rays: $\overrightarrow{BC}$
$\overrightarrow{BA}$
vertex: B
angle: ∠CBA

Identify an angle in each figure shown. Draw a figure for each angle given.

3.

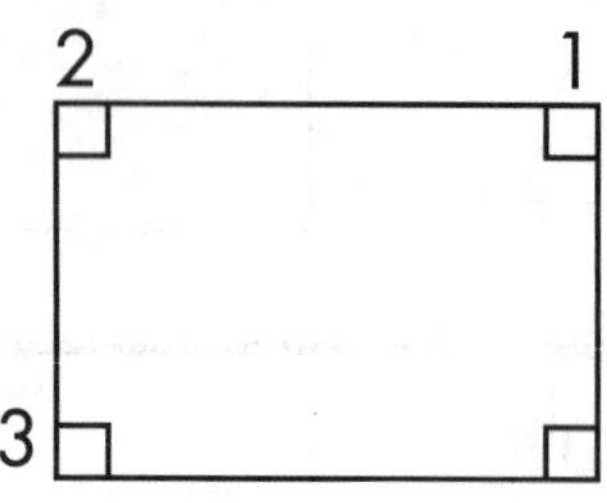

angle: ______

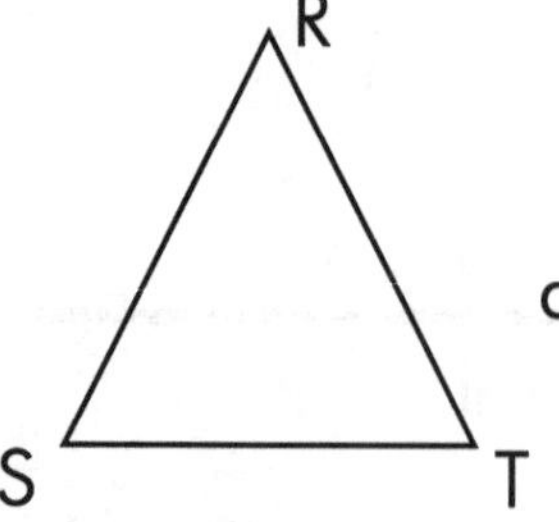

angle: ______

4. ∠XYZ

∠678

NAME ______________________

Lesson 8.2 Parallel and Perpendicular Lines

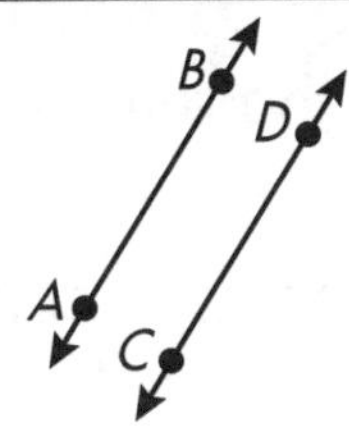

Lines like $\overleftrightarrow{AB}$ and $\overleftrightarrow{CD}$ are called **parallel lines** since they have no points in common. $\overleftrightarrow{AB}$ and $\overleftrightarrow{CD}$ will never intersect.

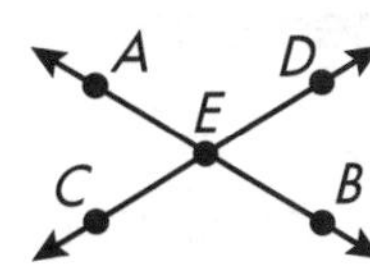

Lines like $\overleftrightarrow{AB}$ and $\overleftrightarrow{CD}$ are called **intersecting lines**. They have one point in common, point E. $\overleftrightarrow{AB}$ intersects $\overleftrightarrow{CD}$ at point E.

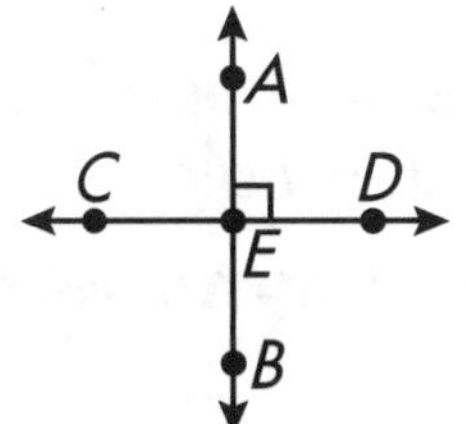

Lines like $\overleftrightarrow{AB}$ and $\overleftrightarrow{CD}$ are called **perpendicular lines**. They form a right angle, shown by the symbol ⌝ in the angle.

Identify each pair of lines as *parallel*, *intersecting*, or *perpendicular*.

Type of Lines

1. 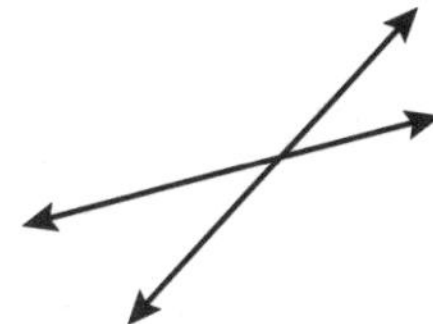 ______

2. 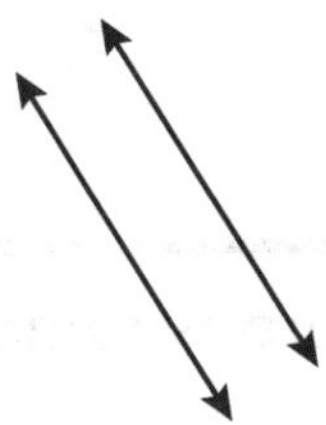 ______

3. 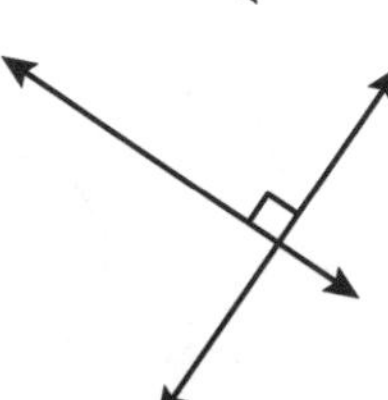 ______

Draw each type of line below.

4. parallel

5. intersecting

6. perpendicular

Identify the lines in the figure that are parallel and perpendicular.

7. A B C D

parallel ______ ______

perpendicular ______ ______ ______ ______

NAME ____________________

Lesson 8.3 Symmetrical Shapes

A figure or shape is **symmetrical** when one-half of the figure is the mirror image of the other half.

A **line of symmetry** divides a figure or shape into two halves that are congruent.

A circle is symmetrical. 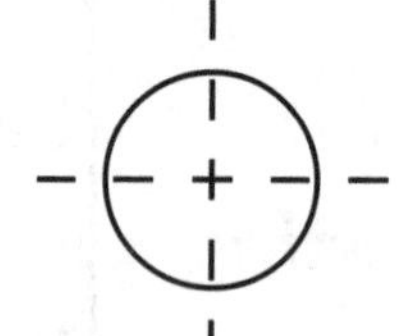 A circle has many lines of symmetry.

State whether the line drawn on each figure is a line of symmetry. Write *yes* or *no*.

	a	b	c	d
1.	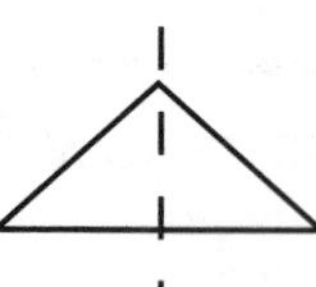 ______	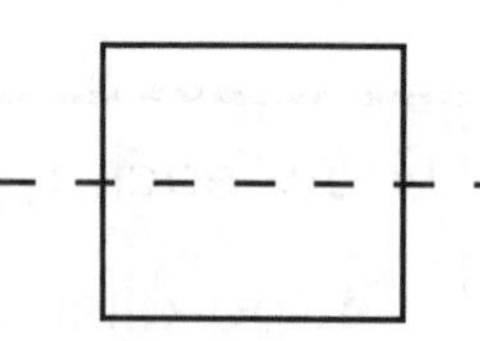 ______	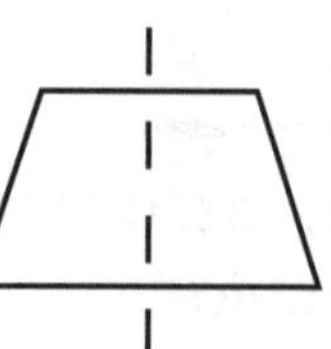 ______	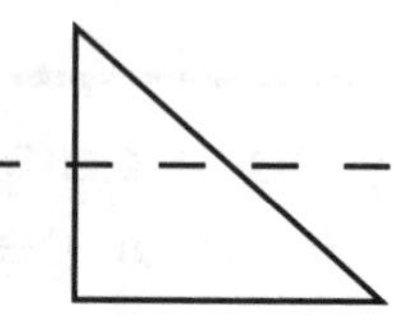 ______
2.	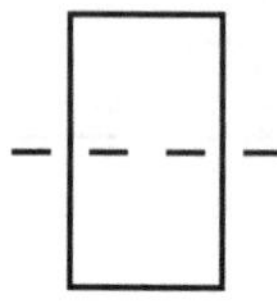 ______	 ______	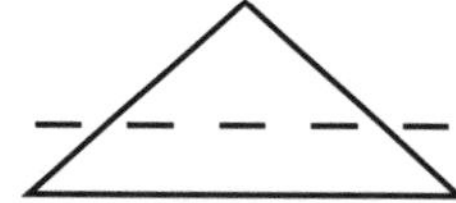 ______	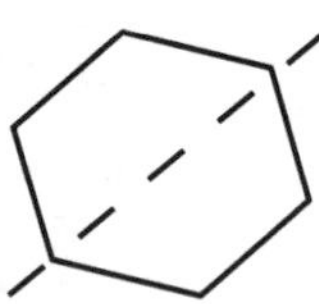 ______

Label each figure as *not symmetrical* or *symmetrical.* If the figure is symmetrical, draw the line (or lines) of symmetry.

3.	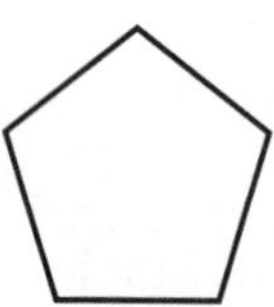 ______	______	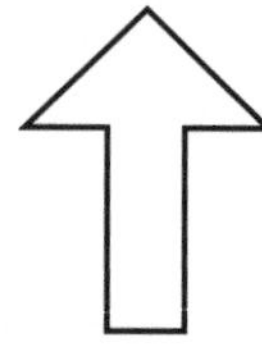 ______	 ______
4.	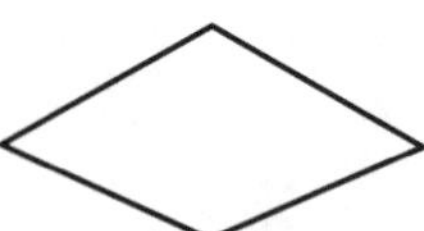 ______	 ______	 ______	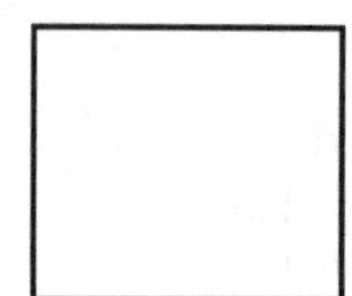 ______

NAME ______________________________

Lesson 8.4 Quadrilaterals

A **quadrilateral** is a polygon with four sides. Some examples are square, rectangle, parallelogram, rhombus, kite, and trapezoid.

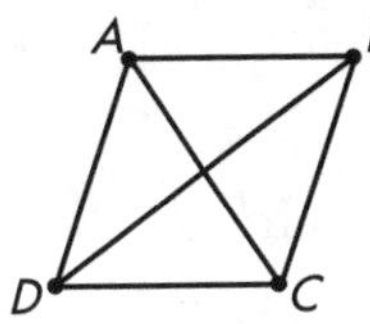

parallelogram
$\angle DAB = \angle BCD$,
$\angle ADC = \angle CBA$
$\overline{AB} = \overline{DC}$, $\overline{AD} = \overline{BC}$
$\overline{AC}$ bisects $\overline{BD}$, $\overline{BD}$ bisects $\overline{AC}$. $\triangle ADC$ is congruent to $\triangle CBA$.

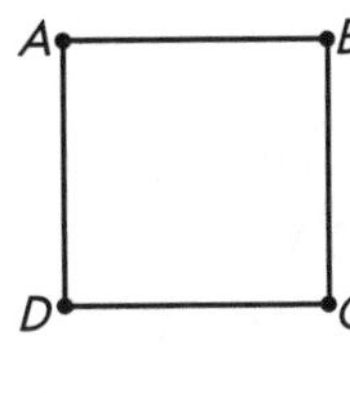

A **square** is a rectangle with 4 sides of same length and all angles equal.
$AB = BC = CD = DA$
$\angle ADC = \angle DCB$, $\angle CBA = \angle BAD = 90°$.

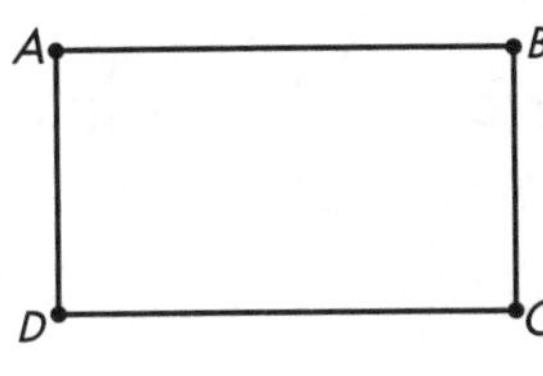

A **rectangle** is a parallelogram with four right angles. Opposite sides are equal. $\overline{AB} = \overline{DC}$, $\overline{AD} = \overline{BC}$, $\angle BAD = \angle ABC = \angle BCD = \angle CDA = 90°$.

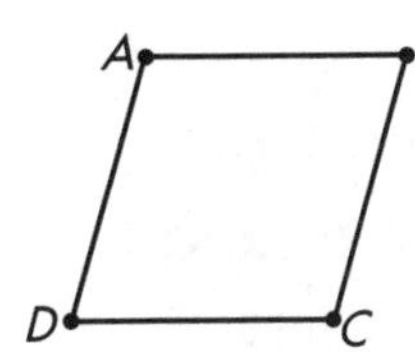

A **rhombus** is a parallelogram with all four sides the same length. Opposite angles are the same measure.

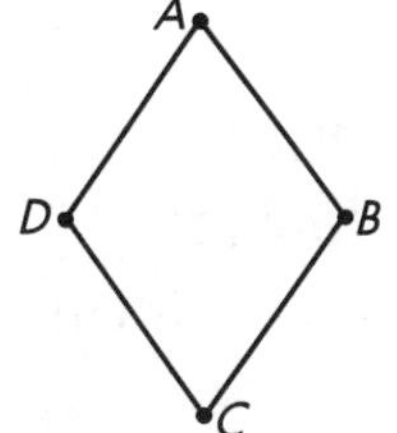

A **kite** has 2 pairs of adjacent sides that are congruent.

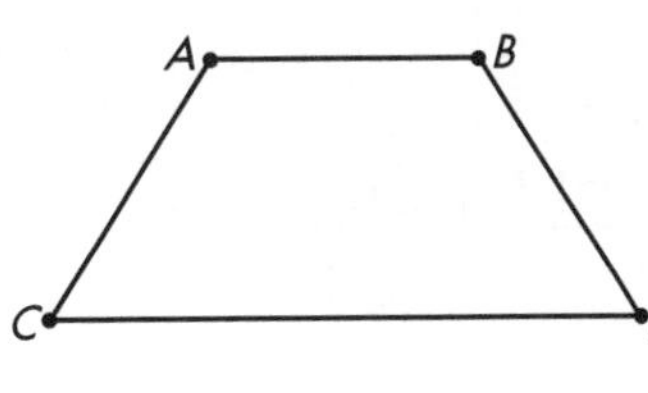

A **trapezoid** has just 2 sides that are parallel.

Identify each quadrilateral.

	a	b	c
1.	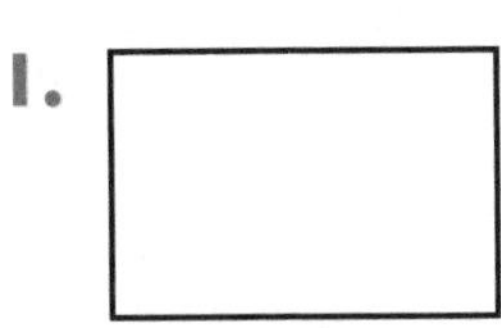 ____________	 ____________	____________
2.	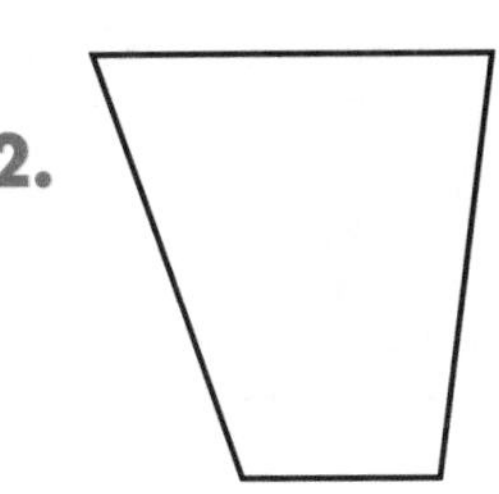 ____________	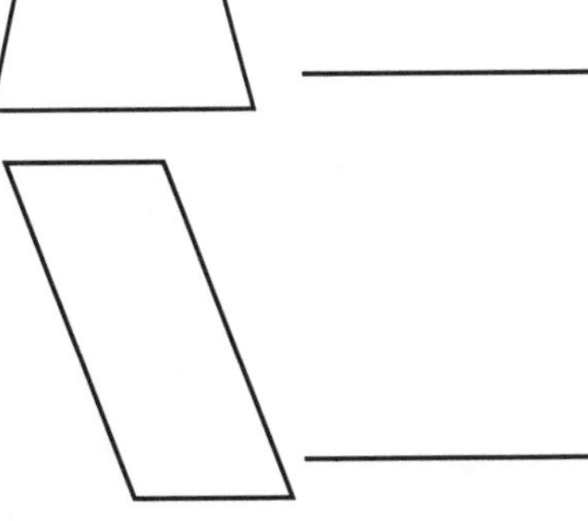 ____________	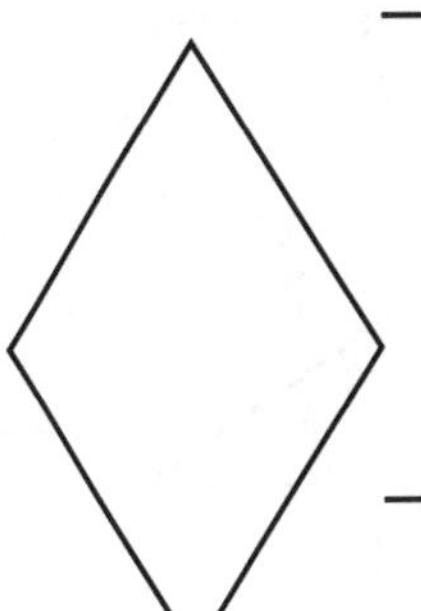 ____________

NAME ______________________________

Lesson 8.5 Triangles

A **triangle** is a polygon with 3 sides. Some examples are equilateral, scalene, isoceles, right, obtuse, and acute.

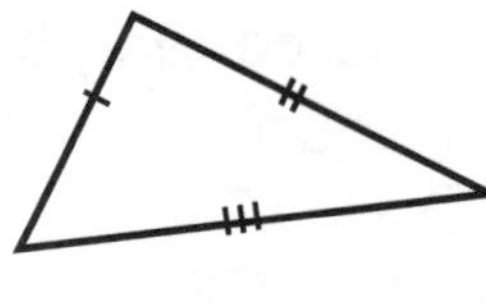

In a scalene triangle, all 3 sides have different lengths. Its angles are also all different.

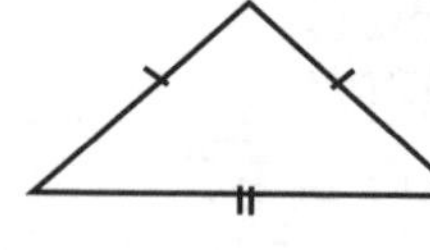

In an isosceles triangle, 2 sides have equal lengths. Two of its angles are also equal.

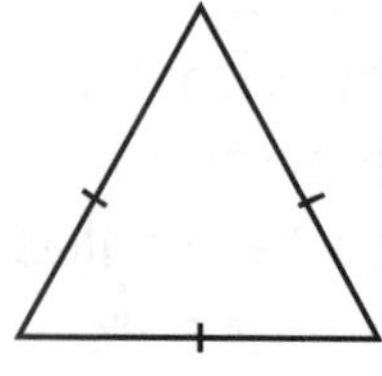

In an equilateral triangle, all 3 sides are the same length. All three angles equal 60°.

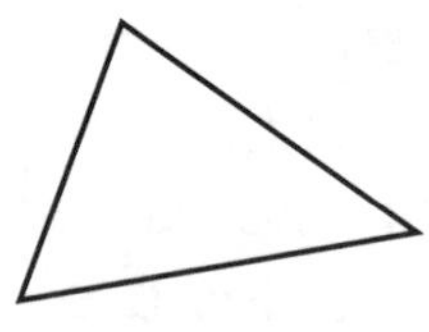

In an acute triangle, all angles are less than 90°.

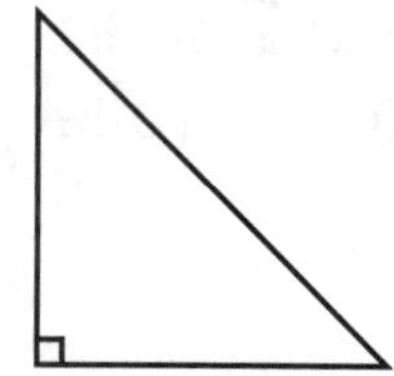

A right triangle has 1 right angle.

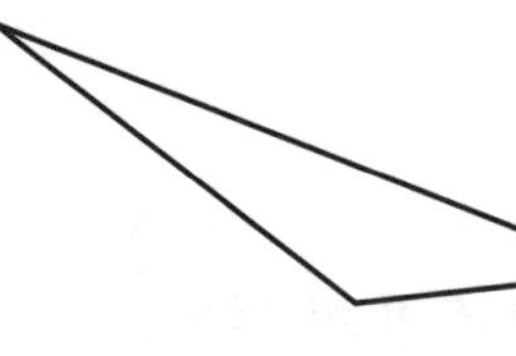

An obtuse triangle has 1 angle that measures more than 90°.

Identify each of the triangles.

	a	b
1.	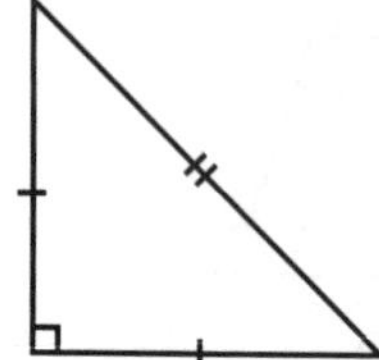 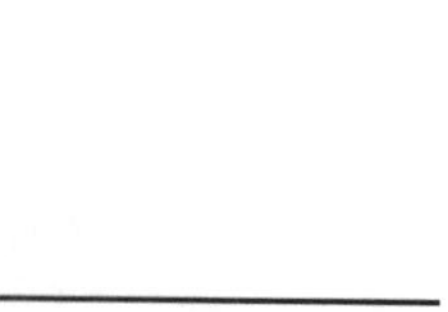 ____________	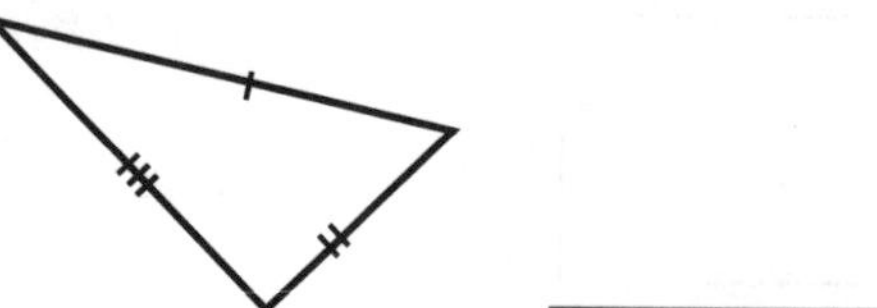 ____________
2.	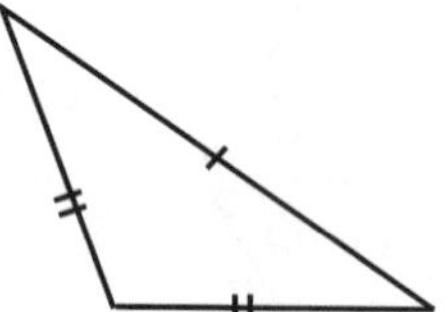 ____________	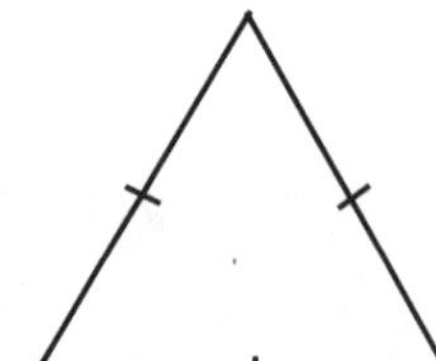 ____________

NAME ______________________

Check What You Learned

Geometry

Draw the line (or lines) of symmetry if the shape is symmetrical.

	a	b	c	d
1.	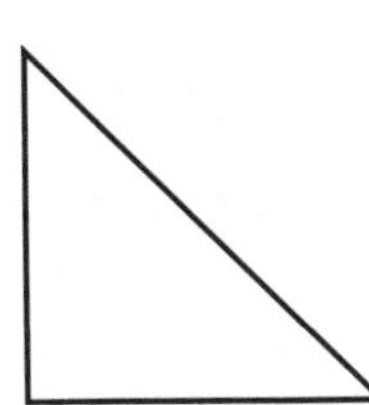			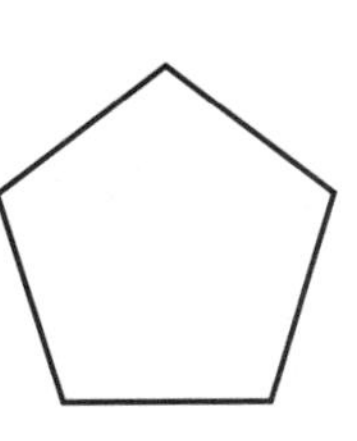

Identify the lines as *perpendicular, parallel,* or *intersecting.*

2. 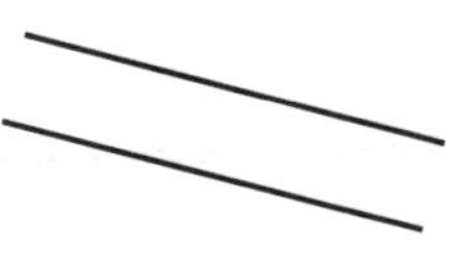

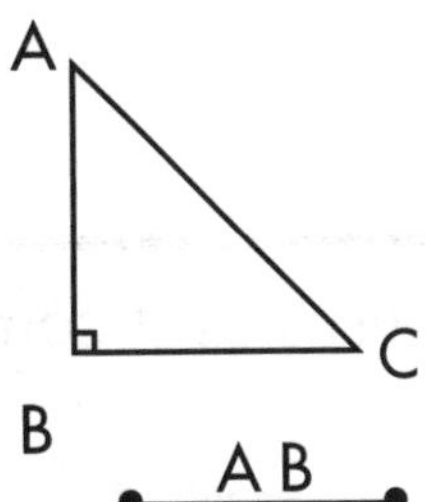

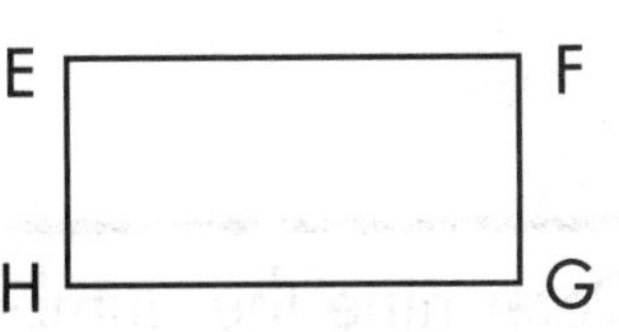

______________ ______________ ______________ ______________

Draw each angle.

	a	b	c
3.	∠QRS	∠567	∠DEF

Identify the quadrilateral.

4. 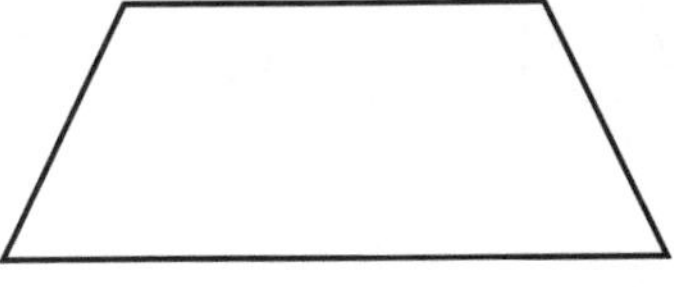

____

Identify the triangle.

5. 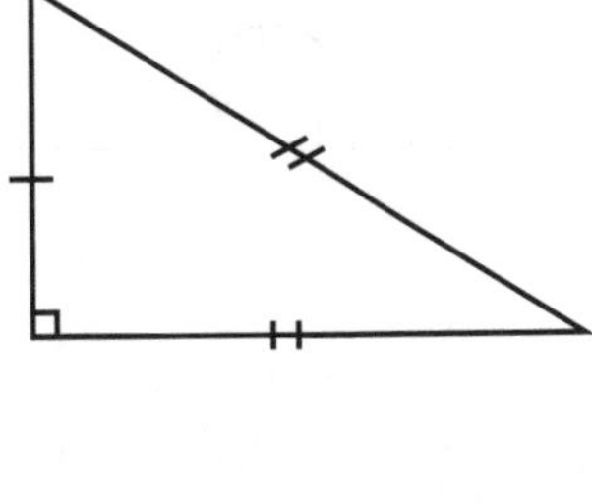

____

CHAPTER 8 POSTTEST

NAME ______________________

Check What You Know

Preparing for Algebra

Complete the number patterns.

	a	b
1.	2, 3, 5, 2, ☐, ☐, ☐	20, 30, 10, 40, 20, ☐, ☐, ☐
2.	75, 50, 25, 10, 75, ☐, ☐, ☐	1, 3, 5, 1, 3, ☐, ☐, ☐

Determine the number patterns and complete.

3.	5, 10, 15, 20, ☐, ☐, ☐	510, 508, 506, ☐, ☐, ☐
4.	4, 8, 16, 32, ☐, ☐, ☐	78, 87, 99, 114, ☐, 153, ☐

Complete the geometric patterns.

5. ○, □, △, ○, ___, ___, ___ ◊, ◊, ⬡, ⬡, ○, ○, ◊, ___, ___, ___

6. cube, sphere, cone, cube, ___, ___, ___ •, ↗, ↕, ↗, •, ___, ___, ___

NAME ____________________

Lesson 9.1 Growing Number Patterns

Increasing Pattern

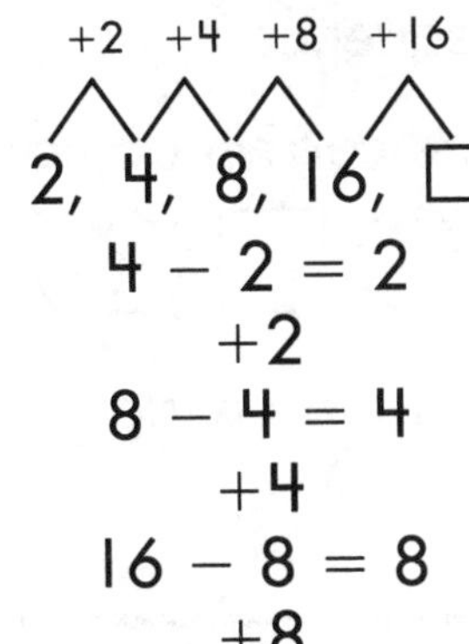

4 − 2 = 2
+2
8 − 4 = 4
+4
16 − 8 = 8
+8

Think: Each number is added to itself to create the increasing pattern.

16 + 16 = 32

The missing number is 32.

To find a missing number in a growing pattern:

1. Find the difference between numbers that are next to each other.
2. The differences in the number series will show the pattern.
3. Add or subtract to find the missing numbers.

Decreasing Pattern

−2 −4 −6 −8 −10 −12

108, 106, 102, 96, 88, 78, □

108 − 106 = 2
−2
106 − 102 = 4
−4
102 − 96 = 6
−6
96 − 88 = 8
−8
88 − 78 = 10
−10

Think: Count by 2s to get the number for the decreasing pattern.

78 − 12 = 66

The missing number is 66.

Complete each pattern.

	a	b
1.	11, 15, 20, 26, 33, □, □	9, 12, 18, 27, □, 54, □
2.	1, 2, 4, 7, □, 16, 22	16, 28, 52, 100, 196, □
3.	5, 7, 11, 17, □, 35, □	158, 156, 152, 146, □, □, □
4.	1128, 1096, 1032, 936, □	88, 110, 154, 220, □, □
5.	460, 450, 430, □, 360, □	923, 915, 904, 890, □, □
6.	180, 176, 168, 156, 140, □	64, 74, 86, 100, □
7.	□, □, 65, 80, 100, 125	□, □, 54, 96, 152, 222

NAME ______________________

Lesson 9.2 Geometric Patterns

What are the next 2 objects in this pattern?

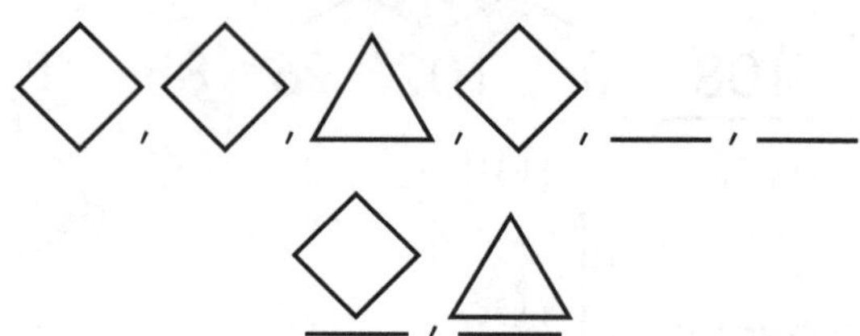

Cross out the object that is not in the correct sequence.

What should be the correct object?

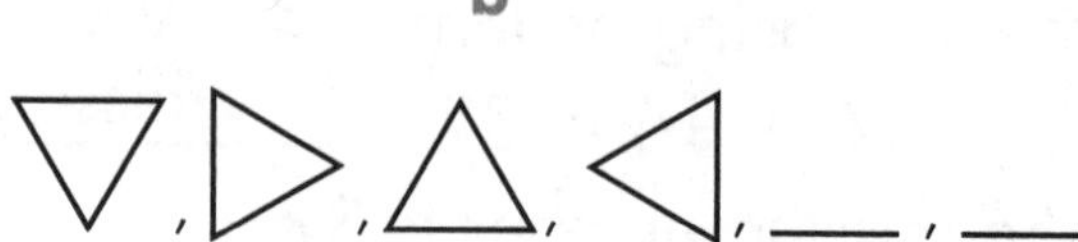

The object should be a hexagon.

Draw the next 2 objects in each pattern.

a | b

1. 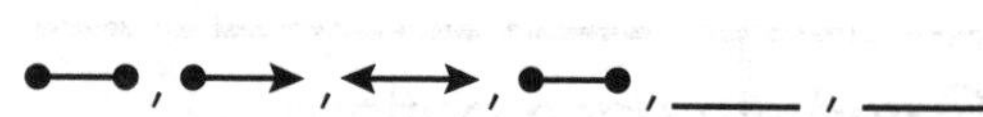

2. 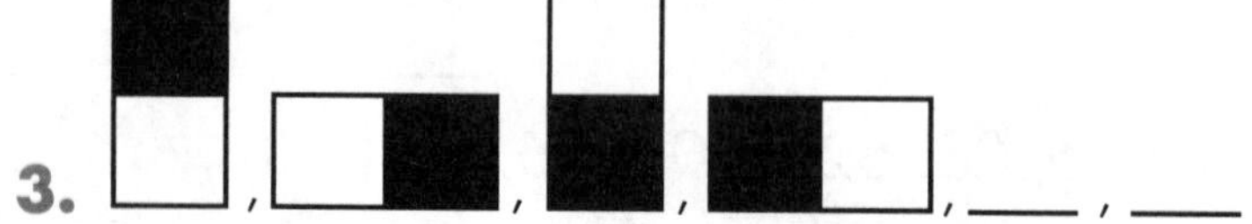

3. 

Find the object that is out of sequence. Cross it out. Draw the correct object on the blank line.

4. 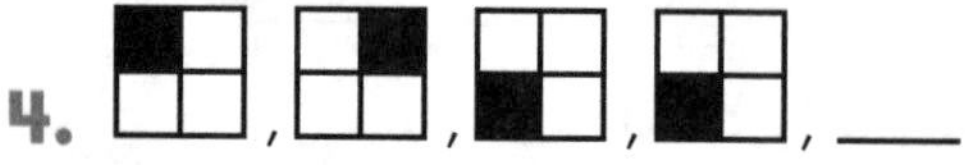 

5. 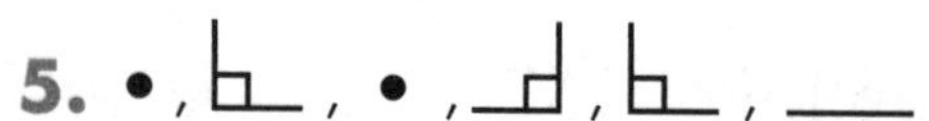 

NAME ___________________________

Check What You Learned

Preparing for Algebra

Complete the number patterns.

	a	b
1.	25, 24, 23, 25, ☐, ☐	256, 257, 256, 258, ☐, ☐
2.	66, 55, 44, ☐, ☐	570, 551, 531, 510, ☐, 465, ☐, ☐
3.	14, 28, 44, 62, ☐, ☐	☐, 26, ☐, 42, 53, 66, 81

Draw the objects that complete the pattern.

4. ⊘, ⦸, ⊘, ⦸, ___, ___   ☐, ☐, ☐, ☐, ☐, ___, ___

5. ⊕, ⊕, ⊕, ⊞, ⊞, ⊞, ⊕, ⊕, ___, ___, ___

NAME ______________________

Final Test Chapters 1–9

Add.

	a	b	c	d	e
1.	21 +15	1932 + 32	718 + 72	247 + 38	1005 + 49
2.	2498 +1832	787 +193	6918 +5832	957 + 98	2950 + 709
3.	25765 + 5403	7864 +3258	20048 7212 + 500	18970 + 2718	50908 7312 + 8903

Subtract.

	a	b	c	d	e
4.	98 − 7	87 − 8	54 − 6	48 − 9	60 − 7
5.	705 −178	6005 − 736	7132 −5600	9568 −7432	900 −445
6.	461 − 32	1353 − 72	777 − 23	2525 − 518	905 − 87

NAME ______________________

Final Test Chapters 1–9

Multiply.

	a	b	c	d	e
7.	78×9	56×8	97×9	48×8	25×9
8.	98×98	78×15	48×36	77×54	83×27
9.	702×6	389×8	215×8	247×2	509×8
10.	7035×2	2003×2	3972×8	5931×4	2450×5

Divide.

11.	3)45	9)72	4)40	5)94	5)85
12.	6)493	3)873	7)875	5)987	8)800
13.	7)2598	2)5282	6)5631	4)9637	5)2515
14.	6)9832	8)5000	5)7004	7)5111	8)9840

NAME ____________________

Final Test Chapters 1–9

Write each number in expanded form.

	a	b
15.	2,337 ______	397 ______
16.	55,608 ______	69, 735 ______

Round each of the numbers to the place of the underlined number.

17.	103,<u>4</u>67 ______	<u>1</u>,785,302 ______
18.	2<u>3</u>,456 ______	5<u>7</u>5 ______

Write >, <, or = to compare the following.

	a	b	c
19.	325 ◯ 225	12,700 ◯ 12,703	164,000 ◯ 146,000

Add or subtract.

20. $\frac{5}{6}+\frac{1}{6}=$ ______ $\frac{7}{12}+\frac{3}{12}=$ ______ $\frac{6}{8}+\frac{4}{8}=$ ______

Complete each equivalent fraction.

21. $\frac{8}{32}=\frac{}{4}$ $\frac{1}{10}=\frac{}{40}$ $\frac{4}{100}=\frac{1}{}$

Write >, <, or = to compare the following.

22. $\frac{3}{8}$ ◯ $\frac{10}{12}$ $\frac{3}{12}$ ◯ $\frac{1}{3}$ $\frac{3}{6}$ ◯ $\frac{4}{8}$

NAME ____________________

Final Test Chapters 1–9

Write the decimal equivalent to the given fraction.

	a	b	c	d
23.	$\frac{8}{10}$ = ______	$\frac{7}{100}$ = ______	$\frac{3}{10}$ = ______	$\frac{6}{10}$ = ______

Complete the following.

	a	b	c
24.	36 in. ______ yd.	7 cm = ______ mm	5 T. = ______ lb.
25.	12 c. = ______ pt.	72 kg = ______ g	132 ft. = ______ yd.
26.	20 m = ______ mm	14 km = ______ m	22 l = ______ mL

Find the perimeter of each shape.

27.

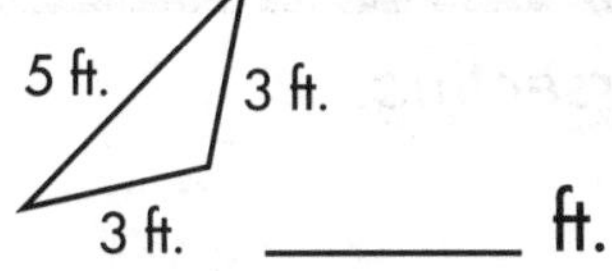

______ ft.

10 in. / 10 in. / 10 in. / 10 in. ______ in.

15 m / 7 m / 7 m / 15 m ______ m

Find the area of each rectangle.

28.

a. 30 ft. × 5 ft. ______ sq. ft.

b. 22 cm × 8 cm ______ sq. cm

c. 10 in. × 30 in. ______ sq. in.

d. 82 mm × 25 mm ______ sq. mm

Solve the problem.

29. Mary is putting new trim and new carpeting in her living room. Her living room is a rectangle, with the long sides measuring 20 feet and the short sides measuring 10 feet. Find the perimeter to see how much trim she will need, and find the area to see how much carpeting Mary will need.

A = ______________ P = ______________

NAME ____________________

Final Test Chapters 1–9

Use a protractor to measure each angle.

	a	b
30.	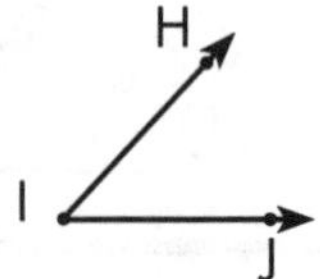 ∠ ______ = ______ °	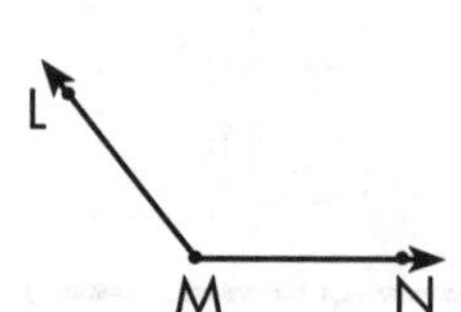 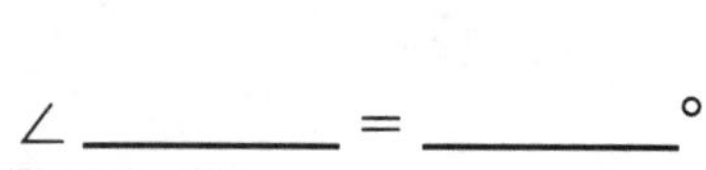 ∠ ______ = ______ °

Draw and label a shape with the angle given.

	a	b	c
31.	∠KLM	∠123	∠OPQ

Identify each pair of lines as *parallel*, *perpendicular*, or *intersecting*.

	a	b	c
32.	 ______	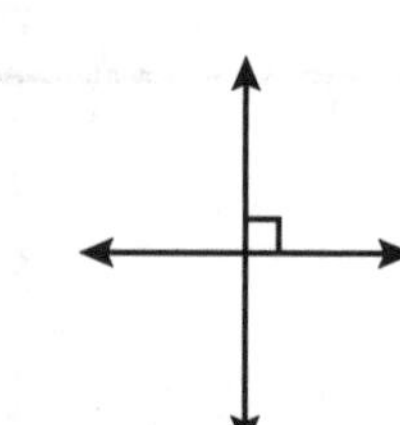  ______	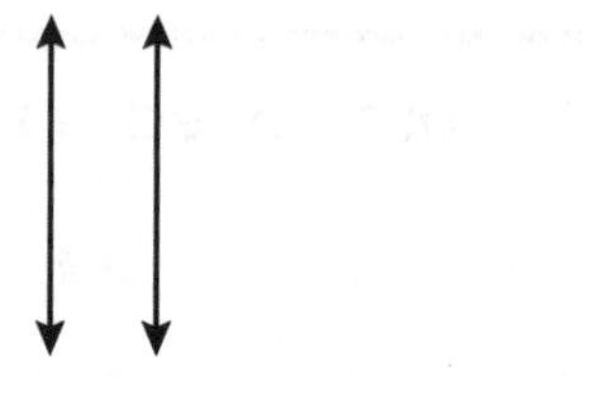 ______

Write the next number in the sequence.

	a	b
33.	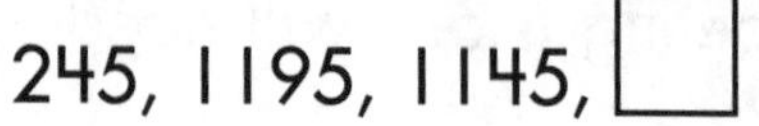 45, 48, 51, ☐	52, 57, 64, 73, 84, ☐, ☐
34.	1245, 1195, 1145, ☐	☐, 25, ☐, 75, 100, ☐, 150, 175

NAME ______________________

Final Test Chapters 1–9

Draw the line (or lines) of symmetry for each figure.

35.

a 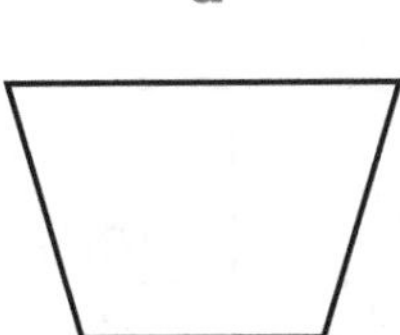

b 

c 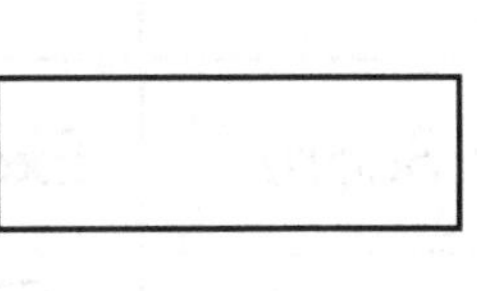

d 

Add or subtract. Write answers in simplest form.

36.

a $3\frac{1}{10} + 4\frac{9}{10} =$ ______

b $6\frac{3}{5} - 4\frac{2}{5} =$ ______

c $3\frac{3}{4} - 1\frac{1}{4} =$ ______

d $1\frac{5}{7} + 6\frac{4}{7} =$ ______

Multiply.

37. $\frac{2}{3} \times 3 =$ ______ $2 \times \frac{7}{12} =$ ______ $7 \times \frac{3}{4} =$ ______ $\frac{4}{7} \times 2 =$ ______

SHOW YOUR WORK

Write each number sentence. Then, solve each problem.

38. The track team ran 10 miles on Saturday. There are 1,760 yards in a mile. How many yards did the track team run?

The track team ran ______ yards.

39. A certain type of blue snake can grow to 28 feet. There are 3 of these snakes in the local zoo. How many feet of blue snakes will the zoo have when these 3 are fully grown?

The zoo will have ______ feet of blue snakes.

38.

39.

NAME ______________________________ DATE ______________

Grade 4 Answers

Scoring Record for Chapter Posttests, Mid-Test, and Final Test

		Performance			
Chapter Posttest	Your Score	Excellent	Very Good	Fair	Needs Improvement
1	____ of 53	50–53	44–50	33–43	22 or fewer
2	____ of 62	56–62	50–55	44–49	45 or fewer
3	____ of 45	43–45	37–42	28–36	27 or fewer
4	____ of 43	40–43	36–39	31–35	30 or fewer
5	____ of 41	40–37	33–39	29–32	28 or fewer
6	____ of 30	27–29	24–26	21–23	20 or fewer
7	____ of 56	52–56	46–53	41–45	40 or fewer
8	____ of 13	13	11–12	9–10	8 or fewer
9	____ of 20	18–19	16–17	14–15	13 or fewer
Mid-Test	____ of 182	170–182	147–169	110–146	109 or fewer
Final Test	____ of 147	133–146	119–132	103–118	102 or fewer

Record your test score in the Your Score column. See where you score falls in the Performance columns. Your score is based on the total number of required responses. If your score is fair or needs improvement, review the chapter material.

Grade 4 Answers

Chapter 1

Pretest, page 5

	a	b	c	d	e	f
1.	38	38	99	25	49	87
2.	67	59	94	98	55	89
3.	83	97	57	98	69	79
4.	19	48	78	89	96	77
5.	41	52	52	64	62	13
6.	22	11	21	52	21	32
7.	10	45	12	71	14	11
8.	31	11	10	33	62	21

Pretest, page 6

9. 36 **10.** 21 **11.** 32 **12.** 21 **13.** 11

Lesson 1.1, page 7

	a	b	c	d	e	f
1.	19	40	39	99	69	97
2.	90	9	19	99	77	80
3.	29	50	99	99	69	90
4.	43	60	99	58	29	70
5.	45	42	49	80	97	79
6.	68	73	39	7	19	77
7.	35	15	87	91	49	62

Lesson 1.2, page 8

	a	b	c	d	e	f
1.	21	23	61	5	70	61
2.	64	21	12	10	31	10
3.	10	90	20	32	17	1
4.	13	11	8	13	7	2
5.	31	71	32	61	71	1
6.	44	10	4	14	11	52
7.	12	51	23	15	22	22

Lesson 1.3, page 9

	a	b	c	d	e	f	g	h
1.	12	11	15	16	17	18	17	14
2.	18	10	13	16	19	20	17	13
3.	20	16	13	16	21	18	16	21
4.	16	19	22	18	14	25	19	21
5.	20	19	25	14	17	17	26	18
6.	19	22	18	19	22	21	20	16

Lesson 1.4, page 10

	a	b	c	d	e	f
1.	51	47	80	31	80	35
2.	91	64	74	81	34	70
3.	91	78	50	90	84	91
4.	63	62	81	70	54	90
5.	90	57	84	91	37	80
6.	68	56	38	85	33	81
7.	82	82	72	96	38	60

Lesson 1.5, page 11

	a	b	c	d	e	f
1.	102	163	194	245	167	139
2.	208	138	220	222	170	276
3.	115	260	144	136	198	105
4.	231	207	230	243	214	166
5.	310	124	242	222	198	227
6.	204	204	222	203	123	231

Lesson 1.6, page 12

	a	b	c	d	e	f
1.	137	115	119	105	116	118
2.	109	118	105	108	119	134
3.	112	146	119	115	143	134
4.	115	109	115	115	107	116
5.	132	119	115	119	126	119
6.	109	136	127	138	133	136
7.	119	128	136	109	125	118

Lesson 1.6, page 13

	a	b	c	d	e	f
1.	79	83	89	69	89	89
2.	82	86	88	86	83	87
3.	77	78	89	89	78	86
4.	34	77	67	79	69	73
5.	89	78	79	86	86	58
6.	88	86	58	79	87	46
7.	69	48	77	49	69	78

Lesson 1.7, page 14

	a	b	c	d	e	f
1.	32 + 47 = 79; 79 − 47 = 32	63 + 19 = 82; 82 − 19 = 63	38 + 24 = 62; 62 − 24 = 38	52 + 47 = 99; 99 − 47 = 52	28 + 15 = 43; 43 − 15 = 28	75 + 15 = 90; 90 − 15 = 75
2.	48 + 27 = 75; 75 − 27 = 48	82 + 10 = 92; 92 − 10 = 82	56 + 38 = 94; 94 − 38 = 56	44 + 27 = 71; 71 − 27 = 44	28 + 27 = 55; 55 − 27 = 28	39 + 32 = 71; 71 − 32 = 39
3.	31 + 59 = 90; 90 − 59 = 31	43 + 18 = 61; 61 − 18 = 43	61 + 29 = 90; 90 − 29 = 61	125 + 17 = 142; 142 − 17 = 125	155 + 38 = 193; 193 − 38 = 155	205 + 69 = 274; 274 − 69 = 205
4.	199 + 14 = 213; 213 − 14 = 199	128 + 33 = 161; 161 − 33 = 128	125 + 50 = 175; 175 − 50 = 125	109 + 32 = 141; 141 − 32 = 109	155 + 27 = 182; 182 − 27 = 155	137 + 29 = 166; 166 − 29 = 137

Grade 4 Answers

Lesson 1.8, page 15

	a	b	c	d	e	f
1.	88	23	47	95	74	98
	−45	−19	−28	−38	−27	−73
	43	4	19	57	47	25
	+45	+19	+28	+38	+27	+73
	88	23	47	95	74	98
2.	38	68	54	49	29	78
	−17	−27	−36	−32	−10	−39
	21	41	18	17	19	39
	+17	+27	+36	+32	+10	+39
	38	68	54	49	29	78
3.	155	132	179	127	141	137
	− 28	− 38	− 82	− 89	− 62	− 52
	127	94	97	38	79	85
	+ 28	+ 38	+ 82	+ 89	+ 62	+ 52
	155	132	179	127	141	137
4.	187	119	192	108	188	164
	− 99	− 20	− 73	− 39	− 90	− 78
	88	99	119	69	98	86
	+ 99	+ 20	+ 73	+ 39	+ 90	+ 78
	187	119	192	108	188	164

Lesson 1.9, page 16

1. 86 **2.** 173 **3.** 207 **4.** 335 **5.** 214

Posttest, page 17

	a	b	c	d	e	f
1.	70	78	52	101	299	100
2.	31	55	306	246	211	204
3.	34	295	165	176	121	82
4.	104	480	64	100	136	87
5.	213	89	23	44	18	28
6.	73	69	189	39	145	11
7.	19	89	19	110	115	58
8.	99	40	25	99	75	63

Posttest, page 18

9. 100 **10.** 112 **11.** 82 **12.** 200 **13.** 295

Chapter 2

Pretest, page 19

1a. 3,000 + 200 + 40 + 5 **1b.** 900 + 70 + 3
1c. 50 + 1
2a. 6,000 + 600 + 70 + 5
2b. 800,000 + 40,000 + 5,000 + 400 + 50
2c. 700 + 90
3a. nine hundred forty-five
3b. four thousand three hundred thirty-two
4a. fifty-two thousand three hundred twenty-one
4b. five hundred twenty-eight thousand four hundred fifty-five
5a. four hundred ninety-five thousand three hundred sixty-two
5b. nine million three hundred sixty-five thousand seven hundred thirty-two
6a. 4,312 > 4,213 **6b.** 95 > 58 **6c.** 408 < 480
7a. 52,650 > 52,560 **7b.** 610 < 672 **7c.** 72 > 62
8a. 52,173 < 520,173 **8b.** 4,675,321 < 4,751,670
8c. 25 < 52
9a. 158,325 = 158,325 **9b.** 652 > 256
9c. 8,910,003 = 8,910,003

Pretest, page 20

	a	b	c
10.	8,000	900	600,000
11.	10,000,000	80	1,700
12.	80,000	930	682,000

	a	b	c	d
13.	90,000	9	900,000	90
14.	9,000,000	9,000	9,000	90,000
15.	900	9	90,000	9,000,000

Lesson 2.1, page 21

1a. 50 + 4 **1b.** 600 + 8
1c. 30 + 2 **1d.** 400 + 20 + 1
2a. 400 + 30 **2b.** 500 + 40 + 9
2c. 70 + 5 **2d.** 600 + 90 + 9
3a. 100 + 30 + 2 **3b.** 700 + 20 + 1
3c. 30 + 9 **3d.** 80 + 7
4a. 900 + 10 + 1 **4b.** 500 + 10 + 3
4c. 100 + 90 **4d.** 70

	a	b	c	d
5.	70	900	6	4
6.	700	60	0	900

a b

7. eighty-five thousand thirty-four
8. eleven thousand nine hundred eighty-seven

Lesson 2.2, page 22

1. one hundred fifty-two thousand seven hundred thirty-one
2. nine hundred eighty-five thousand six hundred eighty-five

	a	b
3.	5	9
4.	9	0
5.	6	9

6a. 600,000 + 50,000 + 3,000 + 400 + 10
6b. 70,000 + 6,000 + 900 + 80 + 2
7a. 60,000 + 2,000 + 500 + 10 + 2
7b. 100,000 + 3,000 + 200 + 50 + 4
8a. 100,000 + 90,000 + 9,000 + 400 + 80 + 2

Grade 4 Answers

8b. 30,000 + 2,000 + 400 + 50 + 1

Lesson 2.3, page 23

1a. 6,420 **1b.** 5,880 **1c.** 45,290
1d. 980 **1e.** 13,940 **1f.** 840
2a. 9,860 **2b.** 26,920 **2c.** 980
2d. 95,650 **2e.** 8,670 **2f.** 29,980
3a. 325,800 **3b.** 49,800 **3c.** 123,700
3d. 24,600 **3e.** 199,800 **3f.** 79,300
4a. 798,800 **4b.** 58,300 **4c.** 9,900
4d. 8,400 **4e.** 10,100 **4f.** 1,987,700
5a. 568,000 **5b.** 94,000 **5c.** 4,000
5d. 12,000 **5e.** 747,000 **5f.** 9,000
6a. 987,000 **6b.** 346,000 **6c.** 98,000
6d. 9,000 **6e.** 75,000 **6f.** 187,000

Lesson 2.3, page 24

1a. 730,000 **1b.** 1,460,000 **1c.** 740,000
1d. 5,550,000 **1e.** 50,000
2a. 180,000 **2b.** 7,740,000 **2c.** 30,000
2d. 480,000 **2e.** 5,640,000
3a. 4,800,000 **3b.** 400,000 **3c.** 9,300,000
3d. 8,000,000 **3e.** 500,000
4a. 8,700,000 **4b.** 1,100,000 **4c.** 400,000
4d. 9,700,000 **4e.** 600,000
5a. 7,000,000 **5b.** 7,000,000 **5c.** 2,000,000
5d. 4,000,000 **5e.** 8,000,000
6a. 2,000,000 **6b.** 4,000,000 **6c.** 7,000,000
6d. 6,000,000 **6e.** 8,000,000

Lesson 2.4, page 25

1a. 105 < 120 **1b.** 52 > 35 **1c.** 10,362 < 10,562
2a. 5,002 > 2,113 **2b.** 713 < 731
2c. 12,317 > 11,713
3a. 115,000 > 105,000 **3b.** 23 < 32;
3c. 142 = 142
4a. 310 > 290 **4b.** 715 < 725
4c. 1,132,700 > 1,032,700
5a. 616 > 106 **5b.** 119,000 < 120,000
5c. 48,112 < 48,212
6a. 823 > 821 **6b.** 2,003,461 < 2,004,461
6c. 7,903 < 9,309
7a. 30 > 25 **7b.** 47,999 > 45,999
7c. 19,900 > 19,090
8a. 111 = 111 **8b.** 386,712 > 386,711
8c. 615 > 614

Lesson 2.4, page 26

1a. 3,647 < 36,647 **1b.** 4,678 < 4,768
1c. 68,035 > 68,025
2a. 4,102,364 < 4,201,364 **2b.** 56,703 > 56,702
2c. 125,125 < 125,150
3a. 90,368 < 90,369 **3b.** 5,654,308 > 5,546,309
3c. 65,003 < 65,013
4a. 4,567,801 > 456,780 **4b.** 7,621 > 7,261
4c. 769,348 > 759,348
5a. 506,708 < 506,807 **5b.** 1,365,333 = 1,365,333
5c. 9,982 > 9,928
6a. 224,364 < 234,364 **6b.** 32,506 > 23,605
6c. 7,850 = 7,850
7a. 3,204,506 < 3,204,606 **7b.** 9,851 > 9,850
7c. 2,000,567 < 2,001,567
8a. 430,632 < 480,362 **8b.** 49,984 = 49,984
8c. 5,640,002 > 5,639,992
9a. 172,302 < 173,302 **9b.** 212,304 = 212,304
9c. 6,886 < 6,896

Posttest, page 27

1a. 1,000,000 + 900,000 + 60,000 + 5,000 + 10 + 2
1b. 600,000 + 90,000 + 3,000 + 100 + 40 + 5
2a. 100,000 + 3,000 + 400 + 50 + 8
2b. 20,000 + 3,000 + 900 + 70 + 2
3a. 400,000 + 70,000 + 1,000 + 400 + 40
3b. 10,000 + 8,000 + 300 + 20 + 1
4a. 90,000 + 8,000 + 400 + 80 + 5
4b. 300,000 + 10,000 + 3,000 + 80 + 2
5a. five thousand twelve
5b. one hundred two
5c. one thousand one hundred forty-one
5d. ninety-nine thousand six hundred twelve
6a. two hundred eighteen
6b. twenty-one thousand eight hundred twelve
6c. seven thousand nine hundred eighty-two
6d. seven hundred sixty-two
7a. four hundred fifty-six
7b. one hundred twenty-three
7c. nine hundred thirty-four thousand seven hundred sixty-three
7d. thirty-seven thousand one hundred three

Posttest, page 28

8a. 2,400,000 **8b.** 760,000 **8c.** 90,000
8d. 2,390,000 **8e.** 630,000
9a. 310,000 **9b.** 8,940,000 **9c.** 430,000
9d. 50,000 **9e.** 2,010,000
10a. 3,000,000 **10b.** 800,000 **10c.** 3,100,000
10d. 900,000 **10e.** 400,000
11a. 500,000 **11b.** 7,700,000 **11c.** 200,000
11d. 6,500,000 **11e.** 500,000
12a. 2,000,000 **12b.** 9,000,000 **12c.** 7,000,000
12d. 5,000,000 **12e.** 7,000,000
13a. 2,000,000 **13b.** 7,000,000 **13c.** 9,000,000
13d. 3,000,000 **13e.** 6,000,000
14a. 24,124 < 24,224 **14b.** 1,975,212 < 1,985,212

Grade 4 Answers

14c. 56,410 > 54,408
15a. 509,712 < 590,172
15b. 2,341,782 = 2,341,782
15c. 976,152 > 967,932
16a. 6,918 > 6,818 **16b.** 49,917 > 49,907
16c. 3,425,556 < 3,524,565
17a. 8,724,100 > 5,724,101
17b. 3,002,019 < 3,002,109 **17c.** 2,418 = 2,418

Chapter 3

Pretest, page 29

	a	b	c	d	e
1.	779	1971	927	3867	6929
2.	5720	310	3588	1248	1877
3.	680	5,437	7,495	9,899	1,980
4.	4,790	3,998	6,737	1,034	6,000
5.	2,503	542	6,408	111	5,905
6.	8,122	1,901	911	6,102	3,967
7.	2,617	2,281	1,163	1,318	22,011
8.	797	5241	320	69,216	9,393

Pretest, page 30

9. 3,994 **10.** 25,994 **11.** 1,398 **12.** 245
13. 448

Lesson 3.1, page 31

	a	b	c	d	e	f
1.	909	750	589	259	788	993
2.	561	408	720	780	598	1,155
3.	983	396	672	810	757	900
4.	980	431	858	1,270	712	309
5.	889	666	543	387	1,300	950
6.	1,014	457	940	584	857	263
7.	1,193	918	1,010	397	1,099	357

Lesson 3.2, page 32

	a	b	c	d	e	f
1.	911	609	1,133	231	4,796	399
2.	4,498	311	290	3,267	103	1,964
3.	1102	190	6,100	524	101	1,069
4.	7,812	281	910	756	151	1,589
5.	108	2,778	3,482	625	4,444	2,692
6.	223	3,747	5,700	1,251	2613	5,086

Lesson 3.3, page 33

	a	b	c	d	e
1.	2,897	5,028	4,210	11,042	8,712
2.	5,499	9,229	9,992	4,330	9,006
3.	6,651	4,622	3,748	3,776	4,145
4.	3,771	5,410	4,028	9,095	7,990
5.	5,115	3,791	5,908	9,595	7,760
6.	10,100	7,983	7,090	2,784	9,919
7.	14,702	3,182	8,134	4,881	6,989

Lesson 3.4, page 34

1. 5,949 **2.** 7,077 **3.** 361 **4.** 131 **5.** 920
6. 3,158

Lesson 3.5, page 35

	a	b	c	d	e
1.	19,115	69,600	33,998	11,123	32,422
2.	65,111	12,990	89,341	13,902	78,921
3.	17	55,198	9,097	8,111	33,690
4.	19,002	34,901	78,064	14,009	10,829
5.	32,899	30,993	11,186	14,219	2,101
6.	4,716	9170	15,000	7,653	7,842
7.	52,108	78,999	11,090	27,680	12,576

Lesson 3.6, page 36

	a	b	c	d	e
1.	730	910	1,068	707	2,563
2.	13,727	840	9,974	1,252	2,312
3.	3,872	18,280	12,189	16,563	1,966
4.	6,762	17,920	4,594	13,675	8,201
5.	7,199	12,820	9,053	16,661	11,930

Lesson 3.7, page 37

	a	b	c	d	e
1.	11,557	24,275	9,099	102,380	3,432
2.	29,850	12,598	22,881	10,018	16,516
3.	8,339	48,390	6,889	50,341	91,001
4.	12,065	11,062	78,186	14,807	40,305
5.	3,860	38,900	13,810	65,237	11,099
6.	17,509	8,217	51,510	4,039	30,583

Lesson 3.8, page 38

1. 8,517 **2.** 15,400 **3.** 64,449 **4.** 4,724
5. 40,851

Lesson 3.9, page 39

	a	b	c	d	e
1.	44,113	76,892	68,111	73,107	12,000
2.	2,727	20,038	99,002	4,559	43,663
3.	57,564	47,408	78,012	46,619	8,973
4.	658	3,476	1,730	1,783	9,041
5.	3,556	6,201	1,085	17,191	786
6.	71,359	1,9788	1,765	9,791	2,190
7.	8,421	1,680	49,106	2,096	7,324
8.	57,829	10,038	14,011	1,818	6,884

Lesson 3.9, page 40

	a	b	c	d	e
1.	7,263	2,470	8,675	15,865	3,507
2.	1,793	19,330	111,175	10,086	208
3.	3,988	42,050	38,966	101	884
4.	6,781	49,059	1,009	250	679
5.	5,163	57,806	791	20,470	2,567

6.	639	25,829	11,819	11,590	7,700
7.	2,075	42,601	4,731	10,389	83,546
8.	10,235	18,354	6,566	7,725	13,906

Lesson 3.10, page 41

1. 111,753 **2.** 2,869 **3.** 14,125 **4.** 4,730
5. 4,240 **6.** 6,002

Posttest, page 42

	a	b	c	d	e
1.	99,013	62,882	1,094	2,600	8,222
2.	26,348	51,609	2,943	13,345	60,012
3.	991	10,050	4,232	111,867	19,991
4.	60,835	1,059	4,024	6,899	28,606
5.	57,818	24,023	659	9,009	18,909
6.	576	337	252	42,753	21,431
7.	56,092	6,228	88,293	8,051	79,874
8.	4,443	5,809	79,231	914	6,812

Posttest, page 43

9. 1,028 **10.** 1,470 **11.** 3,185 **12.** 658
13. 11,808

Chapter 4

Pretest, page 44

	a	b	c	d	e	f
1.	56	75	3,926	255	90	144
2.	14,805	81	4,732	1,056	2,821	744
3.	24,200	1,659	2,200	9,752	2,691	392
4.	17,250	100	1,588	1,875	121	2,916
5.	41,584	1,936	19,266	4,62	5,694	12,832

6. 1, 2, 3, 4, 6, 12; composite
7. 1, 11; prime
8. 1, 2, 4, 5, 10, 20; composite
9. 1, 2, 4, 8, 16, 32; composite

Pretest, page 45

10. 250 **11.** 198 **12.** 8,000
13. 715×3 = a; a = 2,145 **14.** 10×5 = b; b = 50

Lesson 4.1, page 46

1. 1, 2, 4, 8, 16, 32, 64; composite
2. 1, 43; prime
3. 1, 53; prime
4. 1, 2, 3, 4, 6, 8, 9, 12, 18, 24, 36, 72; composite
5. 1, 19; prime
6. 1, 2, 3, 4, 6, 8, 12, 16, 24, 48; composite
7. 1, 2, 11, 22; composite
8. 1, 2, 3, 4, 6, 9, 12, 18, 36; composite
9. 1, 89; prime
10. 1, 31; prime
11. 1, 3, 31, 93; composite
12. 1, 3, 5, 15, 25, 75; composite

Lesson 4.1, page 47

1. 1, 2, 4, 5, 8, 10, 16, 20, 40, 80; composite
2. 1, 5, 11, 55; composite
3. 1, 2, 4, 7, 14, 28; composite
4. . 1, 67; prime
5. 1, 2, 4, 8, 11, 22, 44, 88; composite
6. 1, 73; prime
7. 1, 2, 3, 6, 9, 18, 27, 54; composite
8. 1, 5, 19, 95; composite
9. 1, 2, 3, 6, 9, 18; composite
10. 1, 7, 13, 91; composite
11. 1, 3, 19, 57; composite
12. 1, 13; prime
13. 1, 61; prime
14. 1, 7, 11, 77; composite
15. 1, 3, 11, 33; composite
16. 1, 23; prime

Lesson 4.2, page 48

1. 3 x 4 = a; a = 12
2. 7 x 6 = b; b = 42
3. 6 x $25 = c; c = $150
4. 33 x 5 = d; d = 165
5. 7 x 9 = e; e = 63
6. 4 x 21 = f; f = 84

Lesson 4.3, page 49

	a	b	c	d	e	f
1.	46	71	48	66	70	48
2.	88	86	90	88	36	28
3.	99	75	66	90	40	84
4.	77	20	0	39	60	62
5.	20	82	26	80	60	55
6.	30	77	25	0	66	10
7.	0	50	93	36	80	70

Lesson 4.4, page 50

	a	b	c	d	e	f
1.	292	50	108	260	92	210
2.	38	52	204	270	376	132
3.	288	384	156	136	85	110
4.	198	225	330	171	342	222
5.	165	512	415	343	450	516
6.	360	51	432	225	540	480
7.	279	308	246	288	280	158

Lesson 4.5, page 51

1. 432 **2.** 141 **3.** 368 **4.** 188 **5.** 168 **6.** 115

Lesson 4.6, page 52

	a	b	c	d	e	f
1.	354	1,220	1,120	456	1,400	685
2.	981	474	1,410	1,278	1,740	1,161

Grade 4 Answers

3.	1,675	1,330	3,368	1,809	861	972
4.	2,025	944	1,206	2,988	4,900	796
5.	1,956	568	5,632	1,351	738	1,064
6.	4,224	2,253	1,400	1,110	1,818	5,110

Lesson 4.7, page 53

	a	b	c	d	e	f
1.	726	495	800	713	156	930
2.	861	640	400	651	900	140
3.	968	280	480	900	169	330
4.	770	132	810	288	880	961

Lesson 4.8, page 54

	a	b	c	d	e	f
1.	418	1,312	1,296	675	960	1,694
2.	1,512	2,496	700	2,310	957	6,300
3.	1,311	324	2,079	1,105	1,936	1,800
4.	851	3,458	1,892	221	1,496	2,090

Lesson 4.9, page 55

	a	b	c	d	e	f
1.	9,450	22,134	6,027	16,940	6,270	13,821
2.	4,480	4508	61,916	26,016	24,160	6,750
3.	47,771	37,800	14,256	29,754	59,711	31,836
4.	9,125	21,886	14,784	9,708	44,895	38,014

Lesson 4.10, page 56

	a	b	c	d	e	f
1.	30,751	33,285	35,480	10,528	6,108	26,605
2.	18,886	31,780	22,659	5,448	30,247	13,464
3.	16,254	5,050	30,996	11,045	11,240	29,040
4.	2,887	24,936	8,412	19,044	9,364	48,690
5.	32,432	6,256	20,336	51,384	16,400	20,526
6.	33,608	14,104	47,680	26,190	12,956	5,467

Lesson 4.11, page 57

1. 96 **2.** 396 **3.** 750 **4.** 7,104 **5.** 120 **6.** 80

Posttest, page 58

1a. 288 **1b.** 192 **1c.** 678 **1d.** 272
1e. 1,350 **1f.** 666 **1g.** 186
2a. 484 **2b.** 512 **2c.** 217 **2d.** 6,300
2e. 63 **2f.** 4,844 **2g.** 720
3a. 23,919 **3b.** 728 **3c.** 66 **3d.** 4,347
3e. 5,400 **3f.** 316 **3g.** 4,501
4a. 1,486 **4b.** 4,390 **4c.** 2,691 **4d.** 5,658
4e. 17,886 **4f.** 1,800 **4g.** 22,200
5. 1, 5, 17, 85; composite
6. 1, 59; prime
7. 1, 3, 5, 15; composite
8. 1, 2, 13, 26; composite

Posttest, page 59

9. 460 **10.** 252 **11.** 14,880
12. 35 x 23 = a; a = 805
13. 15 x 12 = b; b = 180

Chapter 5

Pretest, page 60

	a	b	c	d	e
1.	5	7	3	9	3
2.	6	6	9	8	10
3.	9	4	11r2	5	6
4.	2	7	4	3	6
5.	9r6	11	25	87r1	300
6.	15	21	100	9r6	22r2
7.	442r4	20r1	8r6	3r1	938r3

Pretest, page 61

8. 6 **9.** 8 **10.** 4 **11.** 15 **12.** 12 **13.** 47, 6

Lesson 5.1, page 62

	a	b	c	d
1.	100	10	10	2
2.	10	70	10	5
3.	300	10	100	10
4.	60	10	10	50
5.	4	10	20	9

Lesson 5.2, page 63

	a	b	c	d	e	f
1.	7	4	9	6	5	7
2.	9	6	9	4	4	7
3.	9	5	6	8	4	5
4.	8	6	5	7	9	8
5.	6	6	8	5	3	3
6.	7	1	3	2	0	2

	a	b	c	d
7.	5	4	3	9

Lesson 5.3, page 64

	a	b	c	d	e	f
1.	7	9	6	8	9	7
2.	9	6	8	8	9	8
3.	8	6	1	8	0	9
4.	5	2	3	4	7	9
5.	4	5	5	6	3	4
6.	1	3	6	7	2	5

	a	b	c
7.	7	4	8

Lesson 5.4, page 65

	a	b	c	d	e	f
1.	8	5	3	8	4	6
2.	3	7	7	6	9	8
3.	7	8	2	6	4	4
4.	5	6	3	5	2	0

Grade 4 Answers

5.	1	5	6	7	9	7

	a	b	c
6.	7	8	9
7.	9	6	6

Lesson 5.5, page 66

	a	b	c	d	e
1.	7	4	9	7	6
2.	8	5	9	6	9
3.	6	7	4	6	9
4.	9	4	7	8	9
5.	8	3	4	7	5
6.	8	2	9	0	4

Lesson 5.6, page 67

1. 8 **2.** 5 **3.** 9 **4.** 4 **5.** 8 **6.** 7

Lesson 5.7, page 68

	a	b	c	d	e
1.	5r1	8r2	7r3	9r1	5r5
2.	8r2	5r2	6r1	7r1	6r4
3.	3r3	8r1	3r1	9r1	8r1
4.	2r4	6r1	6r1	4r1	9r2

Lesson 5.7, page 69

	a	b	c	d	e
1.	18	15r1	11r2	24	13r2
2.	17r1	32	12r3	12	25
3.	15r3	12r1	11r1	12r5	11
4.	22	28	38r1	19r2	11r5

Lesson 5.8, page 70

	a	b	c	d	e
1.	90	81r3	41r3	43r1	75
2.	92	46r1	62	98r8	21
3.	86r6	45	90r3	73	36r2

Lesson 5.8, page 71

	a	b	c	d	e
1.	128r5	449	141r2	130r1	324
2.	158r1	183	109r8	128r1	197
3.	105r4	112r1	225r1	174	155
4.	261r1	157r3	160r1	111r3	305
5.	108	190r3	217	325	120

Lesson 5.9, page 72

	a	b	c	d	e
1.	1,306	1,720r3	2,065r3	2,121	876r5
2.	1,036r3	2,460r1	1,132r5	179r5	2,937r2
3.	1,582	1,674r3	432r5	1,794	418r2

Lesson 5.9, page 73

	a	b	c	d	e
1.	1,195r3	301r3	780r1	4,565r1	639r2
2.	3,320r1	491r3	1,103r2	538	2,121r2
3.	2,807	7,412	1,129	7,293	4,236r1

Lesson 5.10, page 74

1. 8 **2.** 38 **3.** 58, 7 **4.** 130, 3 **5.** 730

Posttest, page 75

	a	b	c	d	e
1.	6	3	1	8	10
2.	8	6	2	3	7
3.	5	8	6	7	4
4.	7	1	3	9	6
5.	48	29	11r5	10	4r3
6.	9r3	9r1	5r3	9r8	22
7.	2,039r1	183r2	127	5r2	24

Posttest, page 76

8. 8 **9.** 3 **10.** 8 **11.** 65 **12.** 68 **13.** 17

Mid-Test

Mid-Test, page 77

	a	b	c	d	e
1.	25	39	19	39	66
2.	19	74	89	59	79
3.	30	91	81	40	41
4.	43	65	94	81	33
5.	31	72	10	53	32
6.	66	84	9	55	19
7.	69	59	62	82	99
8.	49	93	80	75	65
9.	302	692	209	457	389
10.	889	479	283	462	589

Mid-Test, page 78

11a. 700 + 30 + 2
11b. 30,000 + 2,000 + 100 + 30 + 2
11c. 4,000 + 700 + 90
12a. 1,000 + 3
12b. 2,000,000 + 300,000 + 10,000 + 4,000 + 700 + 30 + 2
12c. 3,000 + 1

	a	b	c
13.	13,600	80,000	2,000,000
14.	4,940	400,000	4,020

15a. 13,702 > 13,207 **15b.** 3,976 < 9362
15c. 932 > nine hundred-one
16a. 26,314 < 260,314 **16b.** 978 = 978
16c. 3,721,460 > 3,710,460

	a	b	c	d	e
17.	875	783	1,088	941	779
18.	3,032	2,350	4,606	9,115	9,810

Mid-Test, page 79

	a	b	c	d	e
19.	29,014	53,010	31,009	54,002	19,147

Grade 4 Answers

20.	8,411	24,810	4,095	28,999	16,949
21.	30,366	1,587	39,087	13,991	8,875
22.	5,150	39,947	10,990	39,559	4,970
23.	91,710	4,464	49,930	8,378	79,967
24.	8,907	29,232	5,444	110,811	83,771

Mid-Test, Page 80

	a	**b**	**c**	**d**	**e**	
25.	56	36	28	48	84	
26.	96	28	88	48	80	
27.	224	141	168	360	153	
28.	336	576	336	175	441	
	a	**b**	**c**	**d**	**e**	**f**
29.	110	242	992	860	500	620
30.	1,875	576	5,412	2,997	1,751	10,716
31.	18,810	16,000	9,353	13,294	46,124	7,581

Mid-Test, Page 81

	a	**b**	**c**	**d**	**e**
32.	9	8	6	8	6
33.	3	7	4	9	10
34.	100	321	103	121	108
35.	90r4	91r2	105	41r1	438
36.	50r8	1,172r3	114	316r1	178r1
37.	100r8	255	1,620r1	111	74r1

Mid-Test, Page 82

38. 36 **39.** 60 **40.** 210 **41.** 18 **42.** 84 **43.** 382

Chapter 6

Pretest, page 83

	a	**b**	**c**	**d**
1.	$\frac{12}{24}$	$\frac{10}{15}$	$\frac{6}{36}$	$\frac{9}{27}$

2. $\frac{1}{5}=\frac{2}{10}$ **3.** $\frac{10}{10}$ or 1 **4.** $\frac{7}{8}$ **5.** $\frac{2}{5}$

6. $\frac{3}{12}$ or $\frac{1}{4}$ **7.** $\frac{1}{4}+\frac{1}{4}=\frac{2}{4}$ **8.** .5 or $\frac{5}{10}$

9. .44 or $\frac{44}{100}$ **10.** .1 or $\frac{1}{10}$

Pretest, page 84

11a. $\frac{48}{100}$ **11b.** $10\frac{2}{6}$ **or** $10\frac{1}{3}$

11c. $13\frac{6}{8}$ or $13\frac{3}{4}$ **11d.** $16\frac{4}{5}$

12a. $3\frac{3}{9}$ or $3\frac{1}{3}$, **12b.** $\frac{22}{100}$

12c. $11\frac{12}{10}$ or $12\frac{2}{10}$ or $12\frac{1}{5}$ **12d.** $3\frac{3}{7}$,

13a. $\frac{32}{9}$ or $3\frac{5}{9}$ **13b.** $\frac{3}{8}$ **13c.** $\frac{8}{7}$ or $1\frac{1}{7}$ **13d.** $\frac{40}{7}$ or $5\frac{5}{7}$

14a. $\frac{15}{10}$ or $\frac{3}{2}$ or $1\frac{1}{2}$ **14b.** $\frac{14}{12}$ or $1\frac{2}{12}$ or $1\frac{1}{6}$

14c. $\frac{42}{11}$ or $3\frac{9}{11}$ **14d.** $\frac{16}{9}$ or $1\frac{7}{9}$

Lesson 6.2, page 85

	a	**b**	**c**	**d**
1.	$\frac{9}{12}$	$\frac{4}{16}$	$\frac{10}{15}$	$\frac{2}{4}$
2.	$\frac{6}{18}$	$\frac{6}{24}$	$\frac{3}{15}$	$\frac{8}{40}$
3.	$\frac{10}{14}$	$\frac{12}{24}$	$\frac{8}{32}$	$\frac{6}{36}$
4.	$\frac{9}{27}$	$\frac{20}{30}$	$\frac{10}{25}$	$\frac{2}{16}$
5.	15	2	12	18
6.	4	16	24	6
7.	40	15	21	10
8.	8	20	27	9

Lesson 6.2, page 86

	a	**b**	**c**
1.	$\frac{1}{4}<\frac{3}{4}$	$\frac{1}{2}=\frac{2}{4}$	$\frac{2}{3}>\frac{1}{2}$
2.	$\frac{7}{10}>\frac{3}{5}$	$\frac{3}{8}<\frac{3}{4}$	$\frac{1}{3}<\frac{5}{8}$
3.	$\frac{1}{5}=\frac{2}{10}$	$\frac{3}{4}>\frac{1}{2}$	$\frac{6}{10}>\frac{2}{5}$

Lesson 6.3, page 87

	a	**b**
1.	$\frac{4}{8} > \frac{2}{10}$	$\frac{1}{5} = \frac{2}{10}$
2.	$\frac{3}{8} < \frac{10}{12}$	$\frac{3}{12} < \frac{1}{3}$
3.	$\frac{2}{8} = \frac{1}{4}$	$\frac{3}{6} = \frac{4}{8}$

Lesson 6.4, page 88

	a	**b**	**c**	**d**	**e**
1.	$\frac{11}{12}$	$\frac{3}{5}$	$\frac{5}{6}$	$\frac{3}{4}$	
2.	$\frac{4}{10}$	$\frac{5}{8}$	$\frac{2}{3}$	$\frac{4}{7}$	
3.	$\frac{4}{5}$	$\frac{9}{12}$	$\frac{9}{10}$	$\frac{4}{5}$	
4.	$\frac{5}{8}$	$\frac{7}{12}$	$\frac{2}{6}$	$\frac{3}{6}$	$\frac{2}{8}$
5.	$\frac{8}{12}$	$\frac{7}{7}$	$\frac{9}{10}$	$\frac{4}{5}$	$\frac{11}{12}$
6.	$\frac{8}{11}$	$\frac{2}{4}$	$\frac{2}{2}$	$\frac{6}{7}$	$\frac{4}{9}$

Lesson 6.5, page 89

	a	**b**	**c**	**d**	**e**
1.	$\frac{8}{12}$	$\frac{4}{10}$	$\frac{2}{4}$	$\frac{1}{7}$	$\frac{1}{5}$
2.	$\frac{2}{10}$	$\frac{1}{12}$	$\frac{2}{5}$	$\frac{3}{10}$	$\frac{4}{8}$
3.	$\frac{6}{10}$	$\frac{2}{11}$	$\frac{7}{9}$	$\frac{2}{5}$	$\frac{2}{9}$
4.	$\frac{2}{7}$	$\frac{4}{12}$	$\frac{0}{9}$	$\frac{4}{12}$	
5.	$\frac{2}{12}$	$\frac{1}{4}$	$\frac{2}{10}$	$\frac{2}{3}$	
6.	$\frac{4}{8}$	$\frac{1}{7}$	$\frac{3}{12}$	$\frac{7}{10}$	

Grade 4 Answers

Lesson 6.6, page 90

1b. $\frac{1}{6} + \frac{1}{6} + \frac{1}{6} + \frac{1}{6} + \frac{1}{6} = \frac{5}{6}$

OR

$\frac{3}{6} + \frac{2}{6} = \frac{5}{6}$

2a. $\frac{1}{12} + \frac{1}{12} + \frac{1}{12} + \frac{1}{12} = \frac{4}{12}$

OR

$\frac{2}{12} + \frac{2}{12} = \frac{4}{12}$

2b. $\frac{1}{8} + \frac{1}{8} + \frac{1}{8} = \frac{3}{8}$

OR

$\frac{2}{8} + \frac{1}{8} = \frac{3}{8}$

Lesson 6.7, page 91

1. $\frac{2}{3}$ **2.** $\frac{1}{4}$ **3.** $\frac{4}{5}$

4. $\frac{4}{8} + \frac{2}{8} = a$, $a = \frac{6}{8}$ or $\frac{3}{4}$

5. $\frac{2}{7} + \frac{3}{7} = b$, $b = \frac{5}{7}$

Lesson 6.8, page 92

	a	b	c
1.	0.3 or $\frac{3}{10}$	0.7 or $\frac{7}{10}$	0.2 or $\frac{2}{10}$

	a	b	c	d
2.	0.2	0.6	0.9	0.4
3.	0.03	0.004	0.08	0.005

4.

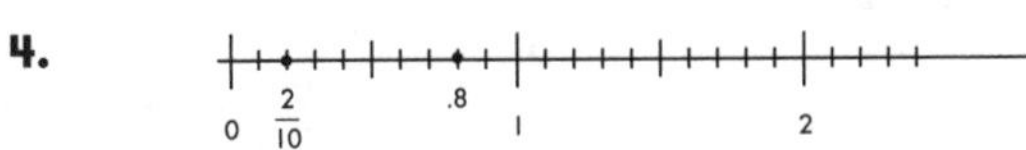

Lesson 6.9, page 93

	a	b	c
1.	29 or $\frac{29}{100}$	$\frac{64}{100}$ or .64	$\frac{98}{100}$ or .98

2.

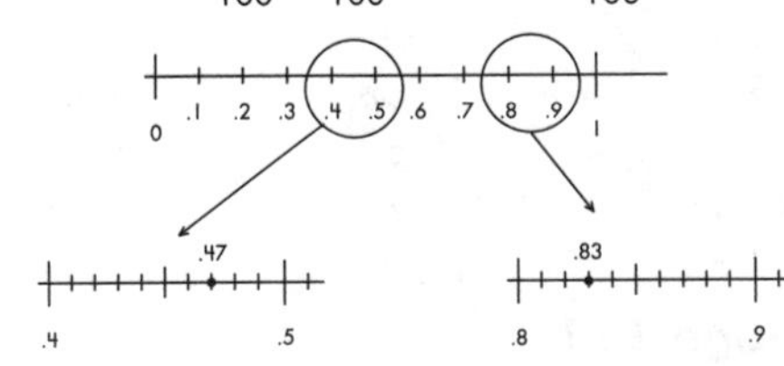

Lesson 6.10, page 94

	a	b	c	d
1.	$\frac{19}{100}$	$\frac{22}{100}$	$\frac{45}{100}$	$\frac{77}{100}$
2.	$\frac{100}{100}$	$\frac{11}{100}$	$\frac{48}{100}$	$\frac{65}{100}$
3.	$\frac{52}{100}$	$\frac{36}{100}$	$\frac{83}{100}$	$\frac{33}{100}$

Lesson 6.11, page 95

	a	b	c	d	e
1.	9	15	$10\frac{1}{3}$	$7\frac{1}{5}$	$11\frac{10}{11}$
2.	$12\frac{1}{5}$	$9\frac{1}{4}$	$5\frac{1}{7}$	$15\frac{1}{2}$	$9\frac{4}{9}$
3.	$7\frac{7}{11}$	8	$12\frac{2}{3}$	$13\frac{3}{4}$	$8\frac{2}{7}$
4.	$10\frac{5}{6}$	$16\frac{4}{5}$	14	$8\frac{2}{3}$	$14\frac{4}{5}$

Lesson 6.12, page 96

	a	b	c	d	e
1.	$2\frac{1}{2}$	$4\frac{1}{7}$	$6\frac{1}{4}$	$4\frac{2}{3}$	$3\frac{1}{4}$
2.	$3\frac{1}{3}$	$2\frac{3}{5}$	$2\frac{1}{5}$	2	$1\frac{5}{9}$
3.	$5\frac{1}{11}$	$1\frac{4}{5}$	1	3	$1\frac{1}{7}$
4.	$1\frac{2}{5}$	$3\frac{3}{7}$	$5\frac{3}{5}$	$7\frac{1}{3}$	$3\frac{1}{9}$

Lesson 6.13, page 97

1. 4 **2.** $8\frac{1}{2}$ **3.** $4\frac{3}{5}$ **4.** $1\frac{3}{4}$ **5.** $\frac{1}{3}$

Lesson 6.14, page 98

1. $6\times(\frac{1}{10})$ or $\frac{1}{10}+\frac{1}{10}+\frac{1}{10}+\frac{1}{10}+\frac{1}{10}+\frac{1}{10}$

2. $2\times(\frac{1}{8})$ or $\frac{1}{8}+\frac{1}{8}$

3. $2\times(\frac{1}{4})$ or $\frac{1}{4}+\frac{1}{4}$

4. $7\times(\frac{1}{3})$ or $\frac{1}{3}+\frac{1}{3}+\frac{1}{3}+\frac{1}{3}+\frac{1}{3}+\frac{1}{3}+\frac{1}{3}$

5. $10\times(\frac{1}{6})$ or $\frac{1}{6}+\frac{1}{6}+\frac{1}{6}+\frac{1}{6}+\frac{1}{6}+\frac{1}{6}+\frac{1}{6}+\frac{1}{6}+\frac{1}{6}+\frac{1}{6}$

6. $5(\frac{1}{12})$ or $\frac{1}{12}+\frac{1}{12}+\frac{1}{12}+\frac{1}{12}+\frac{1}{12}$

Lesson 6.15, page 99

	a	b	c	d
1.	$\frac{3}{8}$	$3\frac{1}{3}$	$1\frac{7}{9}$	$1\frac{1}{7}$
2.	$3\frac{3}{5}$	$1\frac{1}{9}$	$\frac{6}{7}$	$5\frac{1}{4}$
3.	$3\frac{5}{9}$	4	$4\frac{4}{5}$	3
4.	$1\frac{1}{2}$	2	$7\frac{7}{8}$	$3\frac{9}{11}$
5.	$3\frac{1}{9}$	$2\frac{7}{10}$	$1\frac{1}{6}$	$5\frac{5}{7}$

Lesson 6.15, page 100

	a	b	c	d
1.	$1\frac{3}{7}$	$2\frac{2}{5}$	$5\frac{1}{4}$	$1\frac{1}{2}$
2.	$1\frac{1}{7}$	$\frac{3}{4}$	$2\frac{2}{3}$	$\frac{3}{5}$
3.	$2\frac{2}{3}$	2	$1\frac{1}{2}$	$\frac{3}{4}$
4.	$1\frac{7}{8}$	$\frac{2}{3}$	3	$3\frac{8}{9}$
5.	$1\frac{1}{6}$	$2\frac{4}{7}$	$2\frac{1}{2}$	4
6.	$\frac{4}{5}$	$3\frac{1}{3}$	$1\frac{5}{7}$	$1\frac{1}{5}$

Grade 4 Answers

Lesson 6.16, page 101

1. $1\frac{1}{3}$ **2.** $2\frac{1}{12}$ **3.** $\frac{3}{7}$ **4.** 2 **5.** $2\frac{1}{4}$
6. $5\frac{1}{7}$ **7.** $227\frac{1}{4}$

Posttest, page 102

	a	b	c	d
1.	$\frac{15}{25}$	$\frac{6}{18}$	$\frac{9}{18}$	$\frac{10}{40}$
2.	$\frac{1}{5}=\frac{2}{10}$	$\frac{3}{4}>\frac{1}{2}$	$\frac{7}{10}>\frac{3}{5}$	
3.	$\frac{2}{4}$ or $\frac{1}{2}$	$\frac{7}{9}$	$\frac{8}{12}$ or $\frac{2}{3}$	$\frac{2}{10}$ or $\frac{1}{5}$

4. $\frac{1}{5}+\frac{1}{5}+\frac{1}{5}=\frac{3}{5}$

OR

$\frac{2}{5}+\frac{1}{5}=\frac{3}{5}$

5. .08

6. .4

Posttest, page 103

	a	b	c	d
7.	$\frac{65}{100}$	$4\frac{1}{7}$	$7\frac{7}{11}$	$3\frac{1}{9}$
8.	$\frac{33}{100}$	$3\frac{3}{9}$ or $3\frac{1}{3}$	$1\frac{2}{5}$	$8\frac{7}{7}$ or 9
9.	$7\frac{1}{9}$	$2\frac{6}{12}$ or $2\frac{1}{2}$	$1\frac{1}{8}$	$2\frac{6}{11}$
10.	$\frac{3}{4}$	$4\frac{1}{2}$	$1\frac{1}{5}$	$2\frac{8}{10}$ or $2\frac{4}{5}$

Chapter 7

Pretest, page 104

	a	b
1.	1 yd.	2 gal.
2.	8 oz.	1760 yd.
3.	24 in.	5 pt.
4.	1 yd.	4 qt.
5.	20 c	2 qt.
6.	300 sq. yd.; 80 yd.	72 sq. in.; 36 in.
7.	43°	
8.	125°	
9.	79° (Accept answers within 3 degrees above or below actual measurements.)	

Pretest, page 105

10. 12 **11.** 6 ft. **12.** 1,000 lb. **13.** 25 yd.
14. 80 sq. ft.

Pretest, page 106

	a	b
15.	5,000 m	60 L.
16.	600 cm	32,000 g
17.	720 mm	19,000 mL
18.	1,000 mg	1 m
19.	25,000 g	650 mm
20.	17,000 mL	52 m
21.	7 g	25,000 m
22.	20 cm	9 L

23. 1 ¾ miles **24.** 44 ½ miles
25. 72° **26.** 17° **27.** 9°

Pretest, page 107

28. 20,000 **29.** 4,000 **30.** 50 **31.** 39,000

Lesson 7.1, page 108

1.	15	96	216
2.	4	5,280	864
3.	1,000	2	10,560
4.	1	936	4
5.	10	120	2,160
6.	12,320	200	108
7.	52,800	50	72
8.	11	1,800	3
9.	24	1	100
10.	14,080	16	10

Lesson 7.2, page 109

1. 36 **2.** 5 **3.** 21 **4.** 9 **5.** 102,080
6. 281

Lesson 7.3, page 110

	a	b	c
1.	8 qt.	2 qt.	6 pt.
2.	6 gal.	2 c.	20 pt.
3.	7 qt.	7 gal.	28 c.
4.	24 pt.	4 c.	7 pt.
5.	40 qt.	60 c.	9 pt.
6.	48 qt.	11 qt.	8 c.
7.	15 qt.	160 oz.	10 gal.
8.	9 pt.	88 c.	160 pt.
9.	300 pt.	100 pt.	320 oz.
10.	11 c.	4 gal.	100 pt.

Lesson 7.4, page 111

	a	b	c
1.	2 lb.	3 T.	8,000 lb.
2.	640 oz.	4 lb.	12 T.
3.	$\frac{1}{2}$T.	$\frac{1}{2}$lb.	9 T.
4.	128 oz.	192 oz.	$\frac{1}{2}$
5.	10,000		
6.	2		
7.	96,000		
8.	128,000		

9.	1
10.	192,000
11.	20,000

Lesson 7.5, page 112

1. 100 **2.** 30,000 **3.** 30,064
4. 48 **5.** 17,544

Lesson 7.6, page 113

	a	b
1.	20 mm	30 mm
2.	50 mm	90 mm
3.	70 mm	20 mm
4.	50 mm	6 cm
5.	9 cm	110 mm
6.	10 cm	250 mm

Lesson 7.6, page 114

1–7. Answers will vary.

	a	b
8.	6 m	9 km
9.	700 cm	10 km
10.	7,000 m	23,000 m
11.	800 cm	3,200 cm
12.	2,000 m	1,400 cm

Lesson 7.7, page 115

	a	b
1.	400 cm	25,000 mm
2.	21,000 m	250 mm
3.	3,300 cm	14,000 m
4.	1,500 cm	47,000 mm
5.	5,000 m	840 mm
6.	7,500 cm	7,200 cm
7.	10,000 m	66,000 mm
8.	210 mm	19,000 m

Lesson 7.8, page 116

	a	b	c
1.	14 m	30 ft.	28 cm
2.	225 yd.	120 mm	55 ft.
3.	42 km	34 in.	150 yd.

Lesson 7.10, page 117

	a	b	c
1.	180 sq. in.	144 mm	132 sq. ft.
2.	250 sq. yd.	40 sq. in.	480 sq. m
3.	184 sq. yd.	80 sq. km	

Lesson 7.11, page 118

1. 100 ft. **2.** 600 sq. ft. **3.** 4,125 sq. ft. **4.** 52 ft.
5. 625 sq. ft. **6.** 306 ft. **7.** 18,750 sq. ft.

Lesson 7.12, page 119

	a	b	c
1.	3,000 mL	12,000 mL	2,000 mL
2.	75,000 mL	10,000 mL	50,000 mL
3.	13,000 mL	78,000 mL	8,000 mL
4. 75,000 mL		**5.** 7 L	**6.** 12

Lesson 7.13, page 120

	a	b	c
1.	6,000 g	32,000 mg	45,000 g
2.	10,000 mg	42,000 g	9,000 mg
3.	105,000 mg	37,000 mg	12,000 g
4.	183,000 g	18,000 mg	119,000 g
5. 45 g		**6.** 7g	

Lesson 7.14, page 121

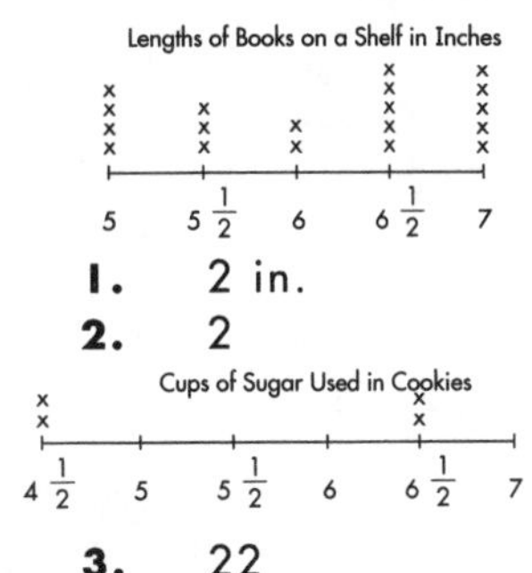

1. 2 in.
2. 2
3. 22

Lesson 7.15, page 122

	a	b
1.	right	acute
2.	obtuse	acute
3.	right	obtuse

Lesson 7.16, page 123

	a	b
1.	∠ABC = 60°	∠GHI = 90°
2.	∠PQR = 110°	∠XYZ = 170°
3.	∠123 = 90°	∠ABC = 30°

4. 90°
5. 50°
6. 125°

Lesson 7.17, page 124

	a	b
1.	45°	75°
2.	68°	75°
3.	88°	28°
4.	17°	145°

Posttest, page 125

	a	b	c
1.	48 in.	80 oz.	4,000 lb.

2.	1 gal.	9 c.	45 ft.
3.	3 mi.	34 c.	5 lb.
4.	44 ft.	45 yd.	
5.	300 sq. ft.	225 sq. in.	
6.	7°	48°	96°

Posttest, page 126

7. $3\frac{1}{2}$ gal. **8.** 200 c. **9.** 8 lb. **10.** 21 in.
11. 20 ft.

Posttest, page 127

	a	b
12.	60 cm	20,500 mm
13.	130 mm	400 cm
14.	37,000 m	15,000 mL
15.	44,000 mg	9,000 g
16.	9,500 cm	2,200 mm
17.	5 km	7,600 cm
18.	5,600 cm	232,000 m
19.	8,650 mm	45,000 mL
20.	267,000 mg	26,000 g
21.	2,000 mL	150 mm
22.	22,000 mm	67,000 m
23.	3 m	3 km
24.	4	
25.	$\frac{6}{8}$ in.	

Posttest, page 128

	a	b	c
26.			
27.	70°	45°.	
28.	40°	20°.	

29. 14,000 **30.** 137,000

Chapter 8

Pretest, page 129

	a	b
1.	∠LMN or ∠NML	∠SRQ or ∠QRS

2. a b c

3. a b c d

4. rectangle
5. right isosceles triangle (accept right, isosceles, or right isosceles)

Lesson 8.1, page 130

	a	b
1.	Rays: $\overrightarrow{QP}$; $\overrightarrow{QR}$ Vertex: Q Angle: ∠PQR or ∠RPQ	Rays: $\overrightarrow{ED}$; $\overrightarrow{EF}$ Vertex: E Angle: ∠DEF or ∠FED

2.

C A B

3. ∠123 ∠RTS or ∠RST or ∠TRS
4a. Answers will vary but may look like:

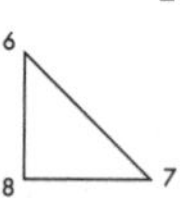

4b. Answers will vary but may look like: 6 8 7

Lesson 8.2, page 131

1. intersecting **2.** parallel **3.** perpendicular
4. **5.** **6.**
7. parallel: AB and DC, AC and BD; perpendicular: AB and AC, AB and BD, CD and DB, CD and CA

Lesson 8.3, page 132

	a	b	c	d
1.	yes	yes	yes	no
2.	yes	no	no	yes
3.	symmetrical	symmetrical	symmetrical	symmetrical
4.	symmetrical	symmetrical	not symmetrical	symmetrical

Lesson 8.4, page 133

	a	b	c
1.	rectangle	trapezoid	rhombus
2.	trapezoid	parallelogram	kite

Lesson 8.5, page 134

	a	b
1.	right	scalene
2.	obtuse or isosceles	equilateral or acute

Posttest, page 135

	a	b	c	d
1.				
2.	parallel	perpendicular	perpendicular	parallel

3. Q R S 5 7 6 D E F
4. trapezoid
5. right

Grade 4 Answers

Chapter 9

Pretest, page 136

	a	b
1.	3, 5, 2	30, 10, 40
2.	50, 25, 10	5, 1, 3
3.	25, 30, 35	504, 502, 500
4.	64, 128, 256	132, 177

5a.

5b.

6a.

6b.

Lesson 9.1, page 137

	a	b
1.	41, 50	39, 72
2.	11	388
3.	25, 47	138, 128, 116
4.	808	308, 418
5.	400, 310	873, 853
6.	120	116
7.	50, 55	12, 26

Lesson 9.2, page 138

1a.

1b.

2a.

2b.

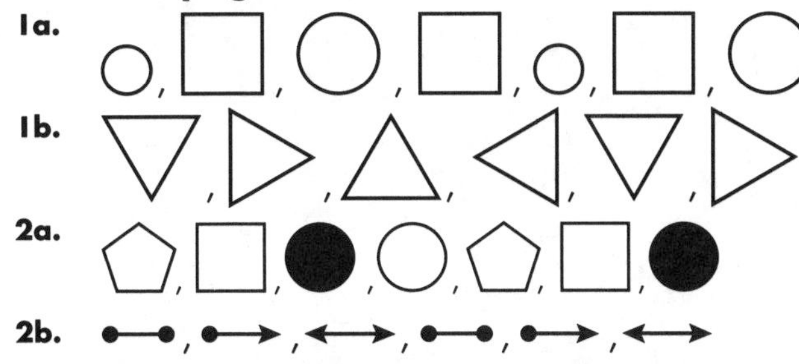

3a.

3b.

4a.

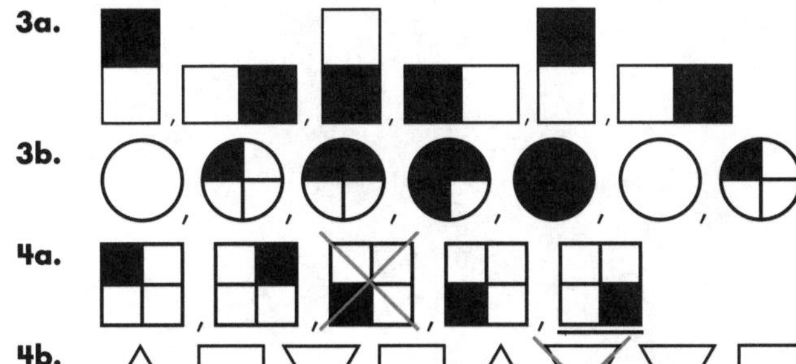

4b.

5a.

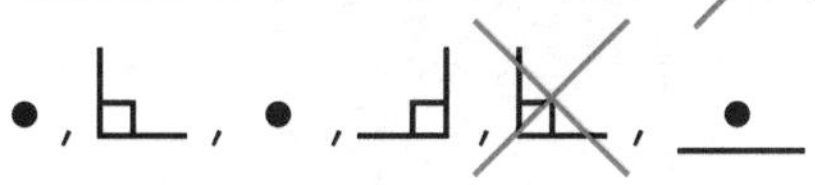

5b.

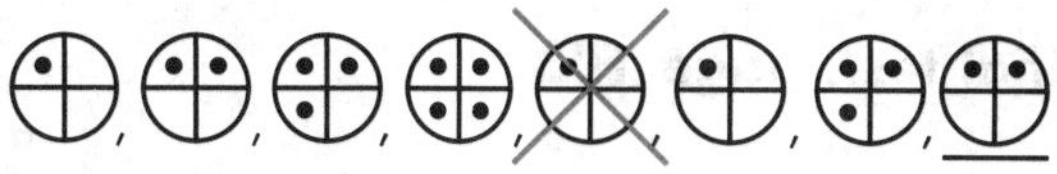

Posttest, page 139

	a	b
1.	24, 23	256, 259
2.	33, 22	488, 441, 416
3.	82, 104	21, 33

5a.

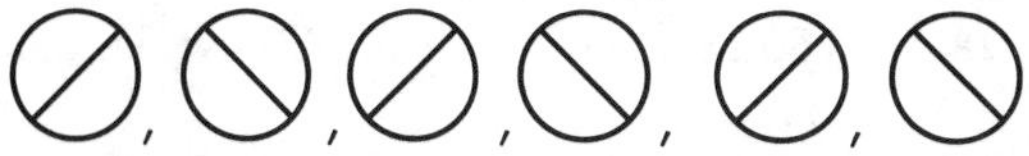

5b.

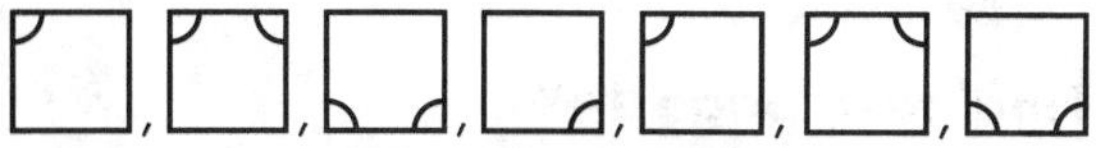

5a.

Final Test

Final test, page 140

	a	b	c	d	e
1.	36	1,964	790	285	1,054
2.	4,330	980	12,750	1,055	3,659
3.	31,168	11,122	27,760	21,688	67,123
4.	91	79	48	39	53
5.	527	5,269	1,532	2,136	455
6.	429	1,281	754	2,007	818

Final test, page 141

	a	b	c	d	e
7.	702	448	873	384	225
8.	9,604	1,170	1,728	4,158	2,241
9.	4,212	3,112	1,720	494	4,072
10.	14,070	4,006	31,776	23,724	12,250
11.	15	8	10	18r4	17
12.	82r1	291	125	197r2	100
13.	371r1	2,641	938r3	2,409r1	503
14.	1,638r4	625	1,400r4	730r1	1,230

Final test, page 142

15a. 2,000 + 300 + 30 + 7

15b. 300 + 90 + 7

16a. 50,000 + 5,000 + 600 + 8

16b. 60,000 + 9,000 + 700 + 30 + 5

	a	b	c
17.	103,500	2,000,000	
18.	23,000	580	
19.	325 > 225	12,700 < 12,703	164,000 > 146,000
20.	6/6 or 1	10/12	1 2/8
21.	1	4	25
22.	3/8 < 10/12	3/12 < 1/3	3/6 = 4/8

Final test, page 143

	a	b	c	d
23.	.8	.07	.3	.6
24.	1 yd.	70 mm	10,000 lb.	
25.	6 pt.	72,000 g	44 yd.	
26.	20,000 mm	14,000 m	22,000 mL	
27.	11 ft.	40 in.	44 m	
28.	150 sq. ft.	176 sq. cm.	300 sq. in.	2,050 sq. mm.

29. Area: 200; Perimeter: 60

Final test, page 144

30a. ∠HIJ or ∠JIH = 47 degrees

30b. ∠LMN or ∠NML = 128 degrees

31. Answers will vary but could include the following:

a 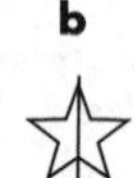

b 

c (O, P, Q)

	a	b	c
32.	intersectiong	perpendicular	parallel
33.	54	97, 112	
34.	1,095	0, 50, 125	

Final test, page 145

	a	b	c	d
35.				
36.	8	$2\frac{2}{5}$	$2\frac{1}{2}$	$8\frac{2}{7}$
37.	2	$1\frac{1}{6}$	$5\frac{1}{4}$	$1\frac{1}{7}$

38. $1{,}760 \times 10 = 17{,}600$

39. $28 \times 3 = 84$